Potato favourites

THE AUSTRALIAN Women's Weekly

Potato favourites

acp books

P.K.R.

contents

wedges, chips and fries

the perfect potato chip

Claimed as pommes frites in France, french fries in America, and chips in Australia and England, the fact remains this humble fried potato is believed to have been invented by the Belgians. What everyone agrees on, is that a perfect chip has to be long, crunchy, golden-brown and possess an earthy, rustic taste enlivened with a hint of oil. Russet burbank (also known as an idaho potato in many cookbooks), with its floury texture and low moisture content, makes the perfect chip, but you can also use spunta, or bintje as we did here.

1kg bintje potatoes, peeled
peanut oil, for deep-frying

1 Cut potatoes lengthways into 1cm slices; cut each slice lengthways into 1cm-wide pieces. Stand potato pieces in large bowl of cold water for 30 minutes to avoid discolouration. Drain; pat dry with absorbent paper.

2 Heat oil in deep-fryer or large saucepan; cook chips, in three batches, about 4 minutes each or until just tender but not browned. Drain on absorbent paper; stand 10 minutes.

3 Reheat oil; cook chips, in three batches, separating any that stick together by shaking deep-fryer basket or with a slotted spoon, until crisp and golden brown. Drain on absorbent paper.

prep + cook time 30 minutes serves 4
nutritional count per serving 14g total fat (2.5g saturated fat); 1208kJ (289 cal); 32.8g carbohydrate; 6g protein; 4g fibre

tips After the first cooking, the chips can stand for several hours before the final deep-frying. Corn oil or vegetable oil can also be used.

Cut the potatoes into 1cm slices, then cut each slice into 1cm-wide pieces; place into cold water.

After the first frying, the chips should be tender, but not brown; drain chips on absorbent paper.

After the second frying, the chips should be crisp and golden brown in colour.

cottage fries

1kg bintje potatoes, peeled
30g butter, chopped
½ cup (125ml) vegetable oil
1 medium brown onion (150g), sliced thickly

1 Using sharp knife, mandoline or V-slicer, slice potatoes into 2mm slices. Stand potato slices in large bowl of cold water for 30 minutes to avoid discolouration. Drain; pat dry with absorbent paper.

2 Heat a third of the butter and a third of the oil in large frying pan; cook a third of the potato and a third of the onion, stirring occasionally, until browned lightly and cooked through. Drain on absorbent paper; cover to keep warm. Repeat, making two more batches, with remaining butter, oil, potato and onion. Return cottage fries to pan; toss to combine, season with freshly cracked black pepper and sea salt, if desired.

prep + cook time 20 minutes (+ standing) **serves** 4
nutritional count per serving 35.2g total fat (7.7g saturated fat); 2040kJ (488 cal); 34.8g carbohydrate; 6.6g protein; 4.5g fibre

Also known as home-fried potatoes, cottage fries are thinly sliced potatoes that can be fried with either onion or green capsicum. You can also use russet burbank or spunta potatoes for this recipe.

gremolata chips

3 medium king edward potatoes (500g), peeled
1 cup (70g) stale breadcrumbs
½ cup finely chopped fresh flat-leaf parsley
½ cup (80g) pine nuts, roasted, chopped finely
2 cloves garlic, crushed
2 tablespoons finely grated parmesan cheese
1 tablespoon finely grated lemon rind
¼ cup (35g) plain flour
1 egg
2 tablespoons milk
2 tablespoons rinsed, drained capers
vegetable oil, for deep-frying
¼ cup (60g) sour cream
100g semi-dried tomatoes

1 Cut potatoes lengthways into four slices. Boil, steam or microwave potato until just tender; drain. Cool.
2 Place breadcrumbs, parsley, nuts, garlic, cheese and rind in medium bowl; stir to combine.
3 Coat each potato slice in flour; shake off excess. Dip each slice in combined egg and milk then toss in breadcrumb mixture; press to coat top and bottom of potato slices. Place on tray, cover; refrigerate 1 hour.
4 Meanwhile, dry capers on absorbent paper. Heat oil in large saucepan; deep-fry capers until crisp. Remove with slotted spoon; drain on absorbent paper.
5 Reheat oil; deep-fry potato slices, in batches, until browned and crisp. Drain on absorbent paper.
6 Serve hot gremolata chips topped with sour cream, semi-dried tomatoes and fried capers.

prep + cook time 35 minutes (+ refrigeration)
makes 12
nutritional count per chip 12.1g total fat (2.6g saturated fat); 815kJ (195 cal); 15.2g carbohydrate; 5.2g protein; 2.7g fibre

Gremolata, a mixture of parsley, garlic and lemon rind, is usually sprinkled over slow-cooked meats, such as osso buco. It's wonderful for adding a refreshing flavour to dishes. You can also use desiree or pink fir apple potatoes for this recipe.

potato skins

You can also use russet burbank or pontiac potatoes for this recipe. Serve potato skins as dippers at your next party or as a snack for the kids to nibble.

1kg desiree potatoes, unpeeled
2 tablespoons olive oil

1 Preheat oven to 220°C/200°C fan-forced.
2 Scrub potatoes well; brush with half the oil. Place potatoes on oven tray; bake, uncovered, about 50 minutes or until tender. Cool.
3 Cut each potato into six wedges; carefully remove flesh, leaving skins intact. Place potato skins, skin-side down, on wire rack over oven tray; brush with remaining oil. Roast, uncovered, about 20 minutes or until crisp. Serve with any of the dips on page 13.

prep + cook time 1 hour 15 minutes (+ cooling)
serves 4
nutritional count per serving 9.4g total fat (1.3g saturated fat); 1041kJ (249 cal); 32.8g carbohydrate; 6g protein; 5g fibre

Carefully scoop out the flesh from the wedges, leaving the skins intact.

Place the potato skins on a wire rack over an oven tray, then brush with the oil.

horseradish and sour cream

Combine 1 finely chopped small brown onion, ¼ cup horseradish cream, ¾ cup light sour cream, ¼ teaspoon sweet paprika and ¼ cup cream in bowl.

makes 1½ cups

nutritional count per tablespoon 4g total fat (2.6g saturated fat); 180kJ (43 cal); 1.3g carbohydrate; 0.6g protein; 0.1g fibre

hummus

Blend or process 300g can rinsed drained chickpeas, 2 tablespoons lemon juice, 1 crushed garlic clove, ¼ cup olive oil, 2 tablespoons tahini and 2 tablespoons water until almost smooth.

makes 1¼ cups

nutritional count per tablespoon 5.8g total fat (0.8g saturated fat); 305 kJ (73 cal); 2.9g carbohydrate; 1.8g protein; 1.3g fibre

tapenade

Blend or process 2 tablespoons roasted pine nuts, 2 cups seeded kalamata olives, 1 crushed garlic clove, 1 tablespoon lemon juice, 1 drained anchovy fillet and ¼ cup olive oil until almost smooth.

makes 1½ cups

nutritional count per tablespoon 4.8g total fat (0.6g saturated fat); 247kJ (59 cal); 3.2g carbohydrate; 0.4g protein; 0.6g fibre

Hot, crisp potato skins are delicious with the dip of your choice; this one is the olive tapenade.

straw potatoes

1kg russet burbank potatoes, peeled
peanut oil, for deep-frying

1 Using sharp knife, mandoline or V-slicer, cut potatoes into 2mm slices; cut each slice into 2mm-wide pieces. Stand potato in large bowl of cold water for 30 minutes to avoid discolouration. Drain; pat dry with absorbent paper.
2 Heat oil in large saucepan; deep-fry potato, in batches, until browned lightly. Drain potato on absorbent paper.

prep + cook time 15 minutes (+ standing) serves 6
nutritional count per serving 8.5g total fat (1.5g saturated fat); 773kJ (185 cal); 21.8g carbohydrate; 4g protein; 2.7g fibre

tip Corn or vegetable oil can be used instead of the peanut oil.

Straw potatoes, as their name implies, are meant to be as thin and crisp as a strand of farmyard straw. They can be served hot or cold, sprinkled with sea salt, if desired. You can also use bintje or spunta potatoes for this recipe.

deep-fried crisps

1kg bintje potatoes, peeled
vegetable oil, for deep-frying

seasoned salt
½ teaspoon sweet paprika
1 teaspoon sea salt flakes
½ teaspoon freshly ground black pepper
pinch cayenne pepper

1 Using sharp knife, mandoline or V-slicer, cut potatoes into 2mm slices. Stand potato pieces in large bowl of cold water for 30 minutes to avoid discolouration. Drain; pat dry with absorbent paper.
2 Meanwhile, make seasoned salt.
3 Heat oil in large saucepan; deep-fry potato, in batches, turning occasionally with slotted spoon, until browned lightly. Drain potato, in single layer, on absorbent paper; sprinkle with seasoned salt.
seasoned salt Combine ingredients in small bowl.

prep + cook time 30 minutes (+ standing) serves 8
nutritional count per serving 6.5g total fat (0.8g saturated fat); 585kJ (140 cal); 16.4g carbohydrate; 3g protein; 2g fibre

After experiencing the flavour and crunchiness of homemade crisps, you will never need to open another packet again. You can also use russet burbank or spunta potatoes for this recipe.

potato wedges

1kg kipfler potatoes, unpeeled, washed
2 tablespoons olive oil

1 Preheat oven to 200°C/180°C fan-forced. Lightly oil two oven trays.

2 Cut each potato into wedges; toss potato wedges and oil in large bowl. Place wedges, in single layer, on trays; roast, uncovered, turning occasionally, about 40 minutes or until crisp and cooked through.

prep + cook time 50 minutes **serves** 4
nutritional count per serving 9.4g total fat (1.3g saturated fat); 1044kJ (249 cal); 32.8g carbohydrate; 6g protein; 5g fibre

Kipfler potatoes must be scrubbed well before being cut into wedges.

Wedges can be coated in egg white rather than oil for a lower-fat version.

The following spice combinations can be tossed with the oil and potato wedges before roasting, if desired. You can also use coliban or sebago potatoes for this recipe. Each of these spice combinations is enough to coat the potato wedges recipe on page 16.

lemon pepper

Combine 1 tablespoon finely grated lemon rind, 1 tablespoon lemon juice and ½ teaspoon freshly ground black pepper in small bowl.

nutritional count per serving (including wedges)
9.4g total fat (1.3g saturated fat); 1049kJ (251 cal); 33g carbohydrate; 6.1g protein; 5.1g fibre

sun-dried tomato flavouring

Combine 1 tablespoon sun-dried tomato pesto, 2 teaspoons tomato sauce and 1 teaspoon sambal oelek in small bowl.

nutritional count per serving (including wedges)
10g total fat (1.4g saturated fat); 1087kJ (260 cal); 33.7g carbohydrate; 6.2g protein; 5g fibre

cajun pepper

Combine ½ teaspoon ground oregano, 2 teaspoons ground cumin, 1 teaspoon hot paprika, ½ teaspoon ground black pepper, 1 teaspoon ground turmeric, 1 teaspoon ground coriander and ¼ teaspoon chilli powder in small bowl.

nutritional count per serving (including wedges)
9.4g total fat (1.3g saturated fat); 1066kJ (255 cal); 33.6g carbohydrate; 6.1g protein; 5.2g fibre

Add your choice of spice to the wedges, then bake, in a single layer, on lightly oiled oven trays.

tempura salt and pepper potatoes with mirin dressing

1 cup (150g) rice flour
1¾ cups (255g) cornflour
1¼ cups (310ml) chilled soda water
500g bintje potatoes, peeled
vegetable oil, for deep-frying

roasted salt and pepper spice
1 teaspoon sichuan peppercorns
1 tablespoon sea salt flakes
2 cinnamon sticks
4 star anise

mirin dressing
1 clove garlic, crushed
1 tablespoon finely chopped fresh ginger
¼ cup (60ml) soy sauce
2 fresh small red thai chillies, sliced thinly
½ cup (125ml) water
¼ cup (55g) sugar
¼ cup (60ml) mirin
1½ tablespoons rice wine vinegar

1 Place rice flour and 1 cup of the cornflour in medium bowl; add soda water, stir until just combined (batter should be lumpy). Cover; stand 30 minutes.

2 Using sharp knife, mandoline or V-slicer, cut potatoes into 2mm slices; dry with absorbent paper.

3 Make roasted salt and pepper spice; make mirin dressing.

4 Heat oil in large saucepan. Dust potato slices, one at a time, with remaining cornflour, then dip in batter. Deep-fry potato, in batches, until browned lightly and crisp; drain on absorbent paper. Sprinkle with roasted salt and pepper spice, serve with mirin dressing.

roasted salt and pepper spice
Preheat oven to 150°C/160°C fan-forced. Sprinkle ingredients evenly onto oven tray; roast 1 hour. Using mortar and pestle, or spice grinder, crush spices until powdered; push spice mixture through fine sieve into small bowl.

mirin dressing
Place ingredients in small saucepan; bring to the boil. Reduce heat; simmer, uncovered, 5 minutes.

prep + cook time 1 hour 30 minutes (+ standing)
serves 4
nutritional count per serving 23.5g total fat (3g saturated fat); 2951kJ (706 cal); 112.2g carbohydrate; 6.9g protein; 3.8g fibre

Contrary to popular belief, tempura did not originate in Japan but was brought to the Land of the Rising Sun by Portuguese missionaries. You can also use purple congo or russet burbank potatoes for this recipe.

potato and parsley wafers

500g bintje potatoes, peeled
1 bunch fresh flat-leaf parsley
vegetable oil, for deep-frying

1 Using sharp knife, mandoline or V-slicer, cut potatoes into 2mm slices.
2 Top half of the potato slices with parsley leaves; top with remaining potato slices, press firmly to seal wafers.
3 Heat oil in large saucepan; deep-fry wafers, in batches, until browned lightly and crisp. Drain on absorbent paper.

prep + cook time 35 minutes **serves** 4
nutritional count per serving 7g total fat (0.9g saturated fat); 602kJ (144 cal); 16.4g carbohydrate; 3g protein; 2g fibre

tip Try layering various herb leaves, such as sage, inside the potato wafers.

These wafers not only look fantastic, but they taste even better. You can also use russet burbank or spunta potatoes for this recipe.

sautéed potatoes

You can also use bintje or russet burbank potatoes for this recipe.

1kg desiree potatoes, unpeeled
2 tablespoons olive oil
50g butter, chopped

Using a sharp knife, cut the unpeeled potatoes into 1cm slices.

Melt the chopped butter with the oil in a large frying pan over medium heat.

1 Cut potatoes into 1cm slices.
2 Heat oil and butter in large frying pan; cook potato, covered, over medium heat, turning occasionally, until browned lightly. Reduce heat; cook, tossing pan to turn potato slices, about 10 minutes or until tender.

prep + cook time 25 minutes **serves** 4
nutritional count per serving 19.6g total fat (8g saturated fat); 1419kJ (339 cal); 32.8g carbohydrate; 6.1g protein; 4g fibre

Toss the potato slices in the frying pan until they are cooked through.

chicken and wedges salad

750g king edward potatoes, unpeeled
1 tablespoon olive oil
4 rindless bacon slices (260g), chopped coarsely
250g cherry tomatoes, halved
2 lebanese cucumbers (260g), seeded, sliced thinly
1 baby cos lettuce, leaves separated
2½ cups (425g) coarsely chopped cooked chicken

herb dressing

1 tablespoon white vinegar
1 tablespoon lemon juice
1 clove garlic, crushed
⅓ cup (80ml) olive oil
2 teaspoons finely chopped fresh basil
2 teaspoons finely chopped fresh oregano

1 Preheat oven to 200°C/180°C fan-forced. Lightly oil oven tray.
2 Cut each potato into six wedges; toss wedges in large bowl with oil. Place wedges, in single layer, on tray; roast, uncovered, about 40 minutes or until browned lightly and tender.
3 Meanwhile, cook bacon in heated oiled large frying pan, stirring, until crisp. Drain on absorbent paper.
4 Make herb dressing.
5 Combine wedges and bacon in large bowl with tomato, cucumber, lettuce and chicken. Add herb dressing; toss gently to combine.

herb dressing
Combine ingredients in screw-top jar; shake well.

prep + cook time 1 hour **serves** 4
nutritional count per serving 41g total fat (8.8g saturated fat); 2830kJ (677 cal); 28.2g carbohydrate; 46.4g protein; 6.4g fibre

You need to buy a large barbecued chicken weighing about 900g for this recipe; discard skin and bones, then chop the meat coarsely. You can also use pontiac or sebago potatoes for this recipe.

lyonnaise potatoes

900g desiree potatoes, peeled, chopped coarsely
1 tablespoon olive oil
2 medium red onions (340g), sliced thinly
3 cloves garlic, crushed
6 rindless bacon slices (390g), chopped coarsely
¼ cup coarsely chopped fresh mint

1 Boil, steam or microwave potato until just tender; drain.

2 Meanwhile, heat half the oil in large frying pan; cook onion and garlic, stirring, until onion softens. Remove from pan.

3 Cook bacon in same pan, stirring, until crisp; drain on absorbent paper.

4 Heat remaining oil in same pan; cook potato, stirring, about 5 minutes or until browned lightly.

5 Return onion mixture and bacon to pan; stir gently to combine with potato. Remove from heat; stir in mint.

prep + cook time 30 minutes **serves** 4
nutritional count per serving 14.2g total fat (4.1g saturated fat); 1630 kJ (390 cal); 34.7g carbohydrate; 28.1g protein; 5.1g fibre

Lyon is seen as one of the gastronomic capitals of the world, and it's no wonder when this French city produces luscious dishes such as this. You can also use ruby lou potatoes for this recipe.

rösti, fritters and patties

the perfect rösti

Rösti, the classic Swiss potato cakes, are best made from a starchy potato, such as spunta or russet burbank, which is grated raw, then immediately cooked fairly slowly in butter. Perfect rösti have a thick crunchy crust and are moist and buttery inside.

1kg russet burbank potatoes, peeled
1 teaspoon salt
80g unsalted butter
2 tablespoons vegetable oil

1 Grate potatoes coarsely into large bowl, stir in salt; squeeze excess moisture from potatoes. Divide potato mixture into eight portions.

2 Heat 10g of the butter and 1 teaspoon of the oil in medium frying pan; spread one portion of the potato mixture over base of pan, flatten with spatula or egg slice to form a firm pancake.

3 Cook, uncovered, over medium heat, until golden brown on underside; shake pan to loosen rösti, then invert onto a large plate. Gently slide rösti back into pan; cook, uncovered, until other side is golden brown and potato centre is tender. Drain on absorbent paper; cover to keep warm.

4 Repeat to make a total of eight rösti.

prep + cook time 25 minutes makes 8
nutritional count per rösti 13g total fat (6.1g saturated fat); 828kJ (198 cal); 16.4g carbohydrate; 3.1g protein; 2g fibre

tips Rösti are best served immediately but can be kept, loosely covered with foil, in a slow oven for up to an hour. Do not grate the potato until ready to cook rösti to avoid discolouring.

Coarsely grate the potatoes into a large bowl; add the salt to draw out any excess liquid.

Flatten the potato mixture with a spatula or egg slice to form a firm round pancake.

Invert the rösti onto a large plate, then gently slide it back into the pan; cook until browned lightly.

potato cakes

1kg sebago potatoes, peeled, chopped coarsely
4 green onions, sliced thinly
4 rindless bacon slices (260g), chopped finely
⅓ cup (40g) coarsely grated cheddar cheese
2 tablespoons sour cream
½ cup (75g) plain flour
50g butter
2 tablespoons olive oil

1 Boil, steam or microwave potato until tender; drain. Mash potato in large bowl until smooth.
2 Meanwhile, cook onion and bacon in heated oiled small frying pan, stirring, until bacon is crisp. Add bacon mixture to potato with cheese and sour cream; stir to combine. Refrigerate mixture 30 minutes.
3 Using floured hands, shape potato mixture into 12 patties; roll in flour, shake off excess.
4 Heat butter and oil in large frying pan; cook potato cakes, in batches, until browned lightly both sides. Serve with lemon wedges, if desired.

prep + cook time 45 minutes (+ refrigeration)
makes 12
nutritional count per cake 11.1g total fat (5.1g saturated fat); 836kJ (200 cal); 15.8g carbohydrate; 8.4g protein; 1.6g fibre

The combination of mashed potato, bacon, onion, cheese and sour cream in these cakes is so good you'll find it hard to stop at one. You can also use lasoda or pink-eye potatoes for this recipe.

hash browns

1kg sebago potatoes, unpeeled
1 small brown onion (80g), chopped finely
2 teaspoons finely chopped fresh rosemary
60g ghee

1 Boil, steam or microwave unpeeled potatoes until just tender; drain. Cool 10 minutes.
2 Peel potatoes; cut into 1cm cubes. Combine potato in large bowl with onion and rosemary.
3 Heat a third of the ghee in medium heavy-based frying pan; place four egg rings in pan. Spoon ¼ cup of the potato mixture into each egg ring; using spatula, spread mixture evenly to fill ring. Cook, pressing frequently with spatula, until browned underneath; carefully turn each ring to brown other side. Drain on absorbent paper; cover to keep warm.
4 Repeat to make a total of 12 hash browns.

prep + cook time 40 minutes **makes** 12
nutritional count per hash brown 5.1g total fat (3.3g saturated fat); 431kJ (103 cal); 11.3g carbohydrate; 2.1g protein; 1.8g fibre

tips Chives, thyme or parsley can be used instead of the rosemary.
A mixture of half olive oil and half melted butter can be used instead of ghee.

Originally called 'hashed brown potatoes', this popular American dish can be eaten at breakfast, lunch or dinner. Ghee is butter that has been clarified to remove the milk solids; this enables it to be heated to a high temperature without burning. You can also use bintje or desiree potatoes for this recipe.

croquettes

1kg coliban potatoes, peeled, chopped coarsely
2 egg yolks
20g butter
½ cup (75g) plain flour
½ cup (60g) finely grated cheddar cheese
⅓ cup (50g) plain flour, extra
2 eggs
2 tablespoons milk
1 cup (100g) packaged breadcrumbs
vegetable oil, for deep-frying

1 Boil, steam or microwave potato until tender; drain. Mash potato in large bowl with yolks, butter, flour and cheese. Cover, refrigerate 30 minutes.
2 Using floured hands, shape heaped tablespoons of the potato mixture into fairly flat fish-finger shapes, dust with extra flour; shake away excess. Dip croquettes, one at a time, in combined eggs and milk, then in breadcrumbs. Refrigerate 30 minutes.
3 Heat oil in large saucepan; deep-fry croquettes, in batches, until browned lightly. Drain croquettes on absorbent paper.

Croquettes can be shaped into flat fish-finger shapes.

Typically croquettes are cylindrical and fairly plump.

prep + cook time 45 minutes (+ refrigeration)
makes 24
nutritional count per croquette 4.6g total fat (1.3g saturated fat); 376kJ (90 cal); 9g carbohydrate; 2.7g protein; 0.8g fibre

tip For a great variation, make pesto and mozzarella croquettes by blending or processing ¾ cup firmly packed fresh basil leaves, 1 tablespoon roasted pine nuts, 1 tablespoon finely grated parmesan cheese, 1 quartered garlic clove, 2 teaspoons lemon juice and 1 tablespoon olive oil, until almost smooth. Add pesto to croquette mixture. Mould croquettes into balls around 5mm-square pieces of mozzarella.

makes 32
nutritional count per croquette 5.6g total fat (1.5g saturated fat); 418kJ (100 cal); 9.1g carbohydrate; 2.9g protein; 0.8g fibre

They may also be shaped into balls and stuffed.

potato puffs

600g coliban potatoes, peeled, chopped coarsely
50g butter, softened
1 clove garlic, crushed
3 rindless bacon slices (195g), chopped finely
½ cup (75g) self-raising flour
1 egg, beaten lightly
2 green onions, chopped finely
¾ cup (90g) finely grated gruyère cheese
vegetable oil, for deep-frying

1 Boil, steam or microwave potato until tender; drain. Mash potato in medium bowl with butter and garlic until smooth; cool.
2 Meanwhile, cook bacon in oiled small frying pan until crisp; drain on absorbent paper. Add bacon, flour, egg, onion and cheese to potato mixture; stir until combined.
3 Heat oil in large deep frying pan; deep-fry level tablespoons of the potato mixture, in batches, until browned. Drain on absorbent paper. Serve with sour cream, if you like.

prep + cook time 45 minutes (+ cooling) **makes** 30
nutritional count per puff 5g total fat (2g saturated fat); 318kJ (76 cal); 4.5g carbohydrate; 3g protein; 0.4g fibre

tip You can substitute 100g crumbled blue cheese for the gruyère, or add 310g can drained corn kernels for a delicious corn-flavoured potato puff.

You can also use nicola or pink-eye potatoes for this recipe.

creamed corn and potato patties

800g sebago potatoes, peeled
1 corn cob (400g), husk and silk removed
2 egg yolks
310g can creamed corn
¾ cup (45g) fresh breadcrumbs
¼ cup finely chopped fresh flat-leaf parsley
¼ cup (35g) plain flour
50g butter
¼ cup (60ml) vegetable oil

1 Boil, steam or microwave potatoes until tender; drain.
2 Meanwhile, using sharp knife, remove kernels from corn cob.
3 Mash potatoes in large bowl until smooth. Add corn kernels, yolks, creamed corn, breadcrumbs and parsley; stir to combine.
4 Using floured hands, shape mixture into 12 patties. Toss patties in flour, shake away excess. Heat a third of the butter and 1 tablespoon of the oil in large frying pan; cook patties, four at a time, until browned both sides.
5 Repeat to make a total of 12 patties.

prep + cook time 1 hour **makes** 12
nutritional count per patty 9.6g total fat (3.2g saturated fat); 811kJ (194 cal); 21g carbohydrate; 4.3g protein; 3.1g fibre

chorizo and potato fritters

2 teaspoons vegetable oil
1 chorizo sausage (200g), chopped finely
1 small brown onion (80g), chopped finely
2 fresh small red thai chillies, chopped finely
2 medium zucchini (240g), grated coarsely
450g bintje potatoes, peeled, grated coarsely
1 small kumara (250g), peeled, grated coarsely
3 eggs, beaten lightly
1 cup (150g) plain flour
1 teaspoon sweet paprika
vegetable oil, for deep-frying

sweet chilli dipping sauce
½ cup (120g) sour cream
2 tablespoons sweet chilli sauce

1 Heat oil in medium frying pan; cook chorizo, onion and chilli, stirring, until onion softens. Add zucchini; cook, stirring, 1 minute. Cool 10 minutes.
2 Meanwhile, make sweet chilli dipping sauce.
3 Combine chorizo mixture in large bowl with potato, kumara, eggs, flour and paprika.
4 Heat oil in large saucepan; deep-fry level tablespoons of the mixture, in batches, until fritters are browned lightly. Drain on absorbent paper. Serve with sweet chilli dipping sauce.

sweet chilli dipping sauce
Combine ingredients in small bowl.

prep + cook time 40 minutes **makes** 40
nutritional count per fritter 4.6g total fat (1.1g saturated fat); 309kJ (74 cal); 5.3g carbohydrate; 2.6g protein; 0.6g fibre

You can also use russet burbank or spunta potatoes for this recipe.

latkes

1kg king edward potatoes, peeled
1 large brown onion (200g), chopped finely
2 eggs, beaten lightly
⅓ cup (55g) polenta
⅓ cup (80ml) vegetable oil
⅓ cup (100g) bottled apple sauce
2 tablespoons sour cream

1 Grate potatoes coarsely; squeeze excess moisture from potato. Combine potato in large bowl with onion, egg and polenta.
2 Using floured hands, shape potato mixture into 12 rounds.
3 Heat oil in large frying pan; cook latkes, in batches, until browned lightly both sides. Drain on absorbent paper; serve topped with apple sauce and sour cream.

prep + cook time 30 minutes makes 12
nutritional count per latke 8.5g total fat (1.9g saturated fat); 677kJ (162 cal); 16.8g carbohydrate; 3.8g protein; 1.8g fibre

Latkes are fried potato pancakes traditionally eaten during Hanukkah because of the significance of oil in this Jewish festival. They're generally made from matzo meal but you can substitute polenta as we have here. You can also use russet burbank or spunta potatoes for this recipe.

perfect salmon patties

Salmon patties are quite easy to make as all the necessary ingredients can usually be found in your pantry. You can also use coliban or nicola potatoes for this recipe.

1kg lasoda potatoes, peeled
440g can red salmon
1 small brown onion (80g), chopped finely
1 tablespoon finely chopped fresh flat-leaf parsley
1 teaspoon finely grated lemon rind
1 tablespoon lemon juice
½ cup (75g) plain flour
1 egg
2 tablespoons milk
½ cup (50g) packaged breadcrumbs
½ cup (35g) stale breadcrumbs
vegetable oil, for deep-frying

Drain the salmon, then remove and discard any flakes of skin or bone.

Using floured hands, shape the salmon mixture into eight patties.

1 Boil, steam or microwave potatoes until tender; drain. Mash potato in large bowl.
2 Drain salmon; discard any skin and bones. Add flaked salmon to potato with onion, parsley, rind and juice; mix well. Cover; refrigerate 30 minutes.
3 Using floured hands, shape salmon mixture into eight patties. Toss patties in flour; shake away excess. Dip patties, one at a time, in combined egg and milk, then in combined breadcrumbs.
4 Heat oil in large saucepan; deep-fry patties, in batches, until browned lightly. Drain patties on absorbent paper.

prep + cook time 40 minutes (+ refrigeration)
makes 8
nutritional count per patty 12.3g total fat (1.8g saturated fat); 1183kJ (283 cal); 33.8g carbohydrate; 7.3g protein; 3.6g fibre

tip Patties can be prepared a day ahead and kept, covered, in the refrigerator.

Dip the patties in combined egg and milk, then in combined breadcrumbs.

smoked trout potato cakes

1kg sebago potatoes, peeled, chopped coarsely
1 clove garlic, crushed
¼ cup (35g) plain flour
2 eggs, beaten lightly
½ cup coarsely chopped fresh coriander
1 teaspoon sambal oelek
1 teaspoon finely grated lime rind
1 tablespoon lime juice
2 whole smoked trout (390g), skin and bones removed, flaked coarsely

1 Preheat oven to 180°C/160°C fan-forced. Lightly oil two oven trays.

2 Boil, steam or microwave potato until tender; drain. Mash potato in large bowl. Add garlic, flour, egg, coriander, sambal, rind and juice; stir to combine. Fold in trout.

3 Using floured hands, shape potato mixture into 12 patties; place patties on trays. Bake, uncovered, in oven about 30 minutes or until potato cakes are browned lightly. Serve with lime wedges and sweet chilli sauce, if you like.

prep + cook time 1 hour 10 minutes **makes** 12
nutritional count per cake 1.9g total fat (0.5g saturated fat); 435kJ (104 cal); 13.2g carbohydrate; 7.8g protein; 1.5g fibre

tip For a more golden colour, quickly pan-fry cakes after removing from oven.

You can also use nicola or pink-eye potatoes for this recipe.

prosciutto and roast capsicum rösti stacks

1 small red capsicum (150g)
1 small yellow capsicum (150g)
⅓ cup (90g) tomato relish
1kg russet burbank potatoes, peeled
80g unsalted butter
2 teaspoons olive oil
8 slices prosciutto (120g)
20g baby spinach leaves
50g parmesan cheese, shaved

1 Preheat grill to hot.

2 Quarter capsicums; remove and discard seeds and membranes. Roast capsicum under grill, skin-side up, until skin blisters and blackens. Cover capsicum with plastic or paper for 5 minutes. Peel away skin, then slice capsicum thinly. Combine capsicum and relish in small bowl.

3 Meanwhile, grate potatoes coarsely; squeeze excess moisture from potato, then divide into eight portions.

4 Heat 10g of the butter in 20cm frying pan; spread one portion of the potato mixture over base of pan, flatten with spatula to form a firm pancake. Cook, uncovered, over medium heat, until golden brown on underside; shake pan to loosen rösti, then invert onto large plate. Gently slide rösti back into pan; cook, uncovered, until other side is golden brown and potato centre is tender. Drain on absorbent paper; cover to keep warm. Repeat to make a total of eight rösti.

5 Heat oil in same frying pan; cook prosciutto until crisp.

6 Place one rösti on each of four serving plates, layer with spinach, prosciutto, capsicum mixture and cheese, then top with a second rösti.

prep + cook time 45 minutes **serves** 4
nutritional count per serving 25.1g total fat (14.5g saturated fat); 1935kJ (463 cal); 39.3g carbohydrate; 17.7g protein; 4.9g fibre

Prosciutto – cured, air-dried ham – is usually sold thinly sliced at your local delicatessen. You can also use spunta or purple congo potatoes for this recipe.

mediterranean potato pancakes

1 tablespoon olive oil
1 medium red onion (170g), chopped coarsely
2 cloves garlic, crushed
1 medium red capsicum (200g), chopped coarsely
1 medium yellow capsicum (200g), chopped coarsely
250g button mushrooms, chopped coarsely
¼ cup (60ml) dry red wine
2 medium egg tomatoes (150g), chopped coarsely
2 x 410g cans crushed tomatoes
200g russet burbank potatoes, peeled, chopped coarsely
¾ cup (110g) plain flour
¼ teaspoon bicarbonate of soda
2 eggs
1¾ cups (430ml) buttermilk
½ cup coarsely chopped fresh basil
½ cup (40g) coarsely grated parmesan cheese

1 Heat oil in large frying pan; cook onion and garlic, stirring, until onion softens. Add capsicums and mushroom; cook, stirring, until vegetables are just tender. Add wine, fresh tomato and 1 can of the undrained tomatoes; bring to the boil. Reduce heat; simmer, uncovered, about 10 minutes or until mixture thickens slightly.
2 Meanwhile, boil, steam or microwave potato until tender; drain. Mash potato in large bowl; cool 10 minutes.
3 Mix combined sifted flour and soda into potato; gradually whisk in combined eggs and buttermilk until batter is smooth. Refrigerate 10 minutes.
4 Preheat oven to 180°C/160°C fan-forced.
5 Heat oiled large frying pan; cook ¼-cup of the batter until browned lightly both sides. Repeat to make a total of 12 pancakes. Cool pancakes 10 minutes.
6 Divide vegetable mixture among pancakes; roll to enclose filling. Place 2 pancakes, seam-side down, in each of six 1½-cup (375ml) baking dishes.
7 Combine remaining can of undrained tomatoes and basil in small bowl; pour over pancakes, sprinkle with cheese. Bake, uncovered, in oven about 15 minutes or until heated through.

prep + cook time 1 hour 15 minutes **serves** 6
nutritional count per serving 7.5g total fat (2.8g saturated fat); 1070kJ (256 cal); 30g carbohydrate; 12.6g protein; 5.3g fibre

Instead of using individual dishes, you could use a single large shallow 3-litre (12-cup) baking dish for this recipe. The cooking time will be the same. You can also use coliban or sebago potatoes for this recipe.

spicy potato pakoras with coriander raita

400g russet burbank potatoes, peeled, cut into 1cm cubes
1 small kumara (250g), peeled, cut into 1cm cubes
1½ cups (225g) besan (see note)
½ teaspoon bicarbonate of soda
¾ cup (180ml) water
2 teaspoons peanut oil
2 cloves garlic, crushed
½ teaspoon ground turmeric
1 teaspoon ground cumin
½ teaspoon dried chilli flakes
2 green onions, chopped finely
vegetable oil, for deep-frying

coriander raita
1 cup (280g) greek-style yogurt
½ cup coarsely chopped fresh coriander
1 teaspoon ground cumin

1 Make coriander raita.
2 Boil, steam or microwave potato and kumara, together, until just tender; drain. Cool 10 minutes.
3 Sift besan and soda into large bowl; gradually add the water, stirring, until batter is smooth.
4 Heat peanut oil in small frying pan; cook garlic, spices and chilli flakes, stirring, until fragrant. Combine garlic mixture in bowl with batter; stir in potato, kumara and onion.
5 Heat vegetable oil in large saucepan; deep-fry tablespoons of mixture, in batches, until pakoras are browned lightly. Drain on absorbent paper; serve with coriander raita.

coriander raita
Combine ingredients in small bowl. Refrigerate until required.

prep + cook time 40 minutes **makes** 24
nutritional count per pakora 4.8g total fat (1.4g saturated fat); 430kJ (103 cal); 11g carbohydrate; 3.9g protein; 1.5g fibre

Besan, a flour made from ground dried chickpeas, is a staple of the Indian kitchen and is used to make roti, chapati and other breads. It is available from health-food stores and many supermarkets. Pakoras are small Indian fritters that can contain vegetables, meat, fish or rice. You can also use desiree potatoes for this recipe.

polenta and parmesan crusted fritters

1kg bintje potatoes, peeled, chopped coarsely
100g prosciutto, chopped finely
1 medium red onion (170g), sliced thinly
150g fennel bulb, sliced thinly
1 egg, beaten lightly
⅓ cup (50g) plain flour
⅓ cup (55g) polenta
½ cup (40g) finely grated parmesan cheese
¼ cup (60ml) olive oil

1 Boil, steam or microwave potatoes until tender; drain. Mash potatoes in large bowl; stir in prosciutto, onion, fennel, egg and flour.
2 Using floured hands, shape potato mixture into eight patties; coat in combined polenta and cheese.
3 Heat oil in medium frying pan; cook patties, in batches, until fritters are browned both sides. Drain on absorbent paper.

prep + cook time 45 minutes **makes** 8
nutritional count per fritter 10.2g total fat (2.5g saturated fat); 1024kJ (245 cal); 27.2g carbohydrate; 9.6 g protein; 3g fibre

You can also use coliban or lasoda potatoes for this recipe.

goat's cheese and potato fritters

600g pontiac potatoes, peeled, chopped coarsely
¼ cup (60ml) pouring cream
¼ teaspoon ground nutmeg
3 eggs, beaten lightly
2 egg yolks, beaten lightly
½ cup (75g) plain flour
250g firm goat's cheese, crumbled
2 tablespoons coarsely chopped fresh flat-leaf parsley
pinch cayenne pepper
vegetable oil, for deep-frying

1 Boil, steam or microwave potatoes until tender; drain. Mash potatoes in large bowl with cream and nutmeg until smooth. Add eggs and egg yolks; using wooden spoon, beat until smooth. Stir in flour, cheese, parsley and pepper.

2 Heat oil in large saucepan; deep-fry level tablespoons of mixture, in batches, until fritters are browned lightly. Drain on absorbent paper.

prep + cook time 30 minutes **makes** 32
nutritional count per fritter 5g total fat (1.9g saturated fat); 305kJ (73 cal); 4.3g carbohydrate; 2.6g protein; 0.4g fibre

You can also use pink-eye or sebago potatoes for this recipe.

potato blini with salsa cruda

200g sebago potatoes, peeled
¾ cup (110g) self-raising flour
½ teaspoon bicarbonate of soda
1 teaspoon finely grated lemon rind
¾ cup (180ml) milk
1 egg
100g butter, melted

salsa cruda

¼ cup (60ml) lemon juice
¼ cup (60ml) extra virgin olive oil
1 clove garlic, crushed
2 medium tomatoes (380g), seeded, chopped finely
½ cup finely chopped fresh flat-leaf parsley
1 small red onion (100g), chopped finely
1 small avocado (200g), chopped finely
1 tablespoon rinsed, drained baby capers

horseradish topping

1 teaspoon horseradish cream
⅓ cup (80g) sour cream
¼ teaspoon sweet paprika

1 Boil, steam or microwave potatoes until tender; drain. Mash potatoes in large bowl; stir in sifted flour and soda.

2 Make a well in the centre of potato mixture; pour in combined rind, milk and egg, stirring, until batter is smooth. Cover; stand 10 minutes.

3 Make salsa cruda; make horseradish topping.

4 Heat large frying pan; brush lightly with a little of the butter. Cook tablespoons of the batter, in five batches, until browned both sides, brushing pan with butter between batches. Transfer blini to wire rack to cool. To serve, top blini with salsa cruda and horseradish topping.

salsa cruda
Combine ingredients in medium bowl.

horseradish topping
Combine ingredients in small bowl.

prep + cook time 1 hour **makes** 25
nutritional count per blini 8.6g total fat (3.9g saturated fat); 435kJ (104 cal); 5.1g carbohydrate; 1.5g protein; 0.5g fibre

You can also use nicola or russet burbank potatoes for this recipe.

sour cream and chive potato pancakes

900g sebago potatoes, peeled
1 medium brown onion (150g), chopped finely
¼ cup finely chopped fresh chives
2 eggs, separated
2 tablespoons plain flour
½ cup (120g) sour cream
⅔ cup (160ml) vegetable oil
80g butter

1 Grate potatoes coarsely; squeeze excess moisture from potato with hands. Combine potato in large bowl with onion, chives, egg yolks, flour and sour cream.
2 Beat egg whites in small bowl with electric mixer until firm peaks form; gently fold into potato mixture.
3 Heat 2 tablespoons of the oil with 20g of the butter in large frying pan; cook heaped tablespoons of the potato mixture, uncovered, until browned both sides. Drain on absorbent paper; cover to keep warm.
4 Repeat to make a total of 20 pancakes.

prep + cook time 35 minutes **makes** 20
nutritional count per pancake 13.9g total fat (4.9g saturated fat); 686kJ (164 cal); 7.3g carbohydrate; 2.5g protein; 0.9g fibre

It is important to squeeze as much excess moisture as possible from the potato so that the pancakes hold their shape while cooking. You can also use russet burbank or spunta potatoes for this recipe.

fetta and spinach stuffed potato balls

450g sebago potatoes, peeled, chopped coarsely
50g butter
⅔ cup (160ml) water
1 teaspoon salt
1 cup (150g) plain flour
2 eggs
vegetable oil, for deep-frying

spinach filling
180g spinach leaves, shredded finely
150g fetta cheese, crumbled

1 Boil, steam or microwave potato until tender; drain. Mash in large bowl; cover to keep warm.
2 Meanwhile, make spinach filling.
3 Melt butter in medium saucepan, add the water and salt; bring to the boil. Remove from heat; immediately stir in flour. Using a wooden spoon, beat until mixture forms a smooth ball. Beat in eggs and potato, beating until smooth.
4 Using floured hands, roll level tablespoons of the dough into balls; use finger to press hole into centre of each ball. Fill holes with level teaspoons of the spinach filling; roll potato balls gently to enclose filling.
5 Heat oil in large saucepan; deep-fry balls, in batches, until browned lightly. Drain on absorbent paper.

spinach filling
Boil, steam or microwave spinach until just wilted; drain. Rinse under cold water; drain. Squeeze as much excess liquid from spinach as possible. Combine spinach in medium bowl with cheese.

prep + cook time 1 hour 10 minutes **makes** 30
nutritional count per ball 5.1g total fat (2g saturated fat); 293kJ (70 cal); 3.8g carbohydrate; 2.1g protein; 0.5g fibre

You can also use lasoda or pink-eye potatoes for this recipe.

roasts, bakes and casseroles

the perfect roast potato

Perfectly roasted potatoes should be crisp and golden brown on the outside, and densely smooth and moist on the inside; full-flavoured and rich but never greasy. Olive oil is better to brush potatoes with than any other oil or butter because it tolerates high oven temperatures and lends its pleasant taste to the potatoes. Gently raking along the length of the peeled potato surface with the tines of a fork assists in crisping. Don't crowd potatoes on the oven tray because they will brown unevenly, and make certain the oven has reached the correct temperature before the tray goes in. Other varieties good for roasting are kipfler, lasoda and pink-eye.

6 pontiac potatoes (1.3kg), peeled, halved horizontally
2 tablespoons light olive oil

1 Preheat oven to 220°C/200°C fan-forced. Lightly oil oven tray.
2 Boil, steam or microwave potatoes 5 minutes; drain. Pat dry with absorbent paper; cool 10 minutes.
3 Gently rake rounded sides of potatoes with tines of fork; place potatoes in single layer, cut-side down, on oven tray. Brush with oil; roast, uncovered, in oven about 50 minutes or until potatoes are browned and crisp.

prep + cook time 1 hour 10 minutes serves 4
nutritional count per serving 9.4g total fat (1.3g saturated fat); 1246kJ (298 cal); 42.6g carbohydrate; 7.8g protein; 5.2g fibre

Pat the potato halves dry with an absorbent paper towel after the initial 5-minute cooking.

Gently rake the potato's surface with the tines of a fork to assist in crisping.

Place the potatoes in a single layer on an oven tray before brushing with the oil.

potatoes anna

1.2kg ruby lou potatoes, peeled
100g butter, melted

1 Preheat oven to 240°C/220°C fan-forced. Lightly oil shallow 2-litre (8-cup) 26cm-round baking dish.
2 Using sharp knife, mandoline or V-slicer, slice potatoes into 2mm slices; pat dry with absorbent paper. Place a single layer of potato, slightly overlapping, into baking dish; brush with a little of the butter. Continue layering remaining potato and butter, cover dish with foil; bake 20 minutes.
3 Remove foil; use metal spatula to press down on potato.
4 Reduce oven temperature to 220°C/200°C fan-forced; bake, uncovered, about 30 minutes or until top is crisp and browned lightly. Cut into wedges to serve.

prep + cook time 1 hour 10 minutes **serves** 6
nutritional count per serving 13.9g total fat (9g saturated fat); 1066kJ (255 cal); 26.3g carbohydrate; 4.9g protein; 3.2g fibre

In the late 1800s, French chef Adolphe Dugléré devised this dish in honour of Anna Deslions, a courtesan who entertained clients in a private dining room within his restaurant. You can also use coliban potatoes for this recipe.

hasselback potatoes

This Swedish version of roasted potatoes produces a wonderfully crisp crust and makes an excellent accompaniment to roasts. You can also use ruby lou potatoes for this recipe.

6 desiree potatoes (1.1kg), peeled, halved horizontally
40g butter, melted
2 tablespoons olive oil
¼ cup (25g) packaged breadcrumbs
½ cup (60g) finely grated cheddar cheese

Place a chopstick on chopping board along each side of the potato half.

Slice the potato to the chopsticks to prevent cutting all the way through.

1 Preheat oven to 180°C/160°C fan-forced.
2 Place one potato half, cut-side down, on chopping board; place a chopstick on board along each side of potato. Slice potato thinly, cutting through to chopsticks to prevent cutting all the way through. Repeat with remaining potato.
3 Coat potato halves in combined butter and oil in medium baking dish; place, rounded-side up, in single layer. Roast, uncovered, 45 minutes, brushing frequently with oil mixture. Continue roasting without brushing about 15 minutes or until potatoes are cooked through.
4 Sprinkle combined breadcrumbs and cheese over potatoes; roast, uncovered, in oven about 10 minutes or until topping is browned lightly.

prep + cook time 1 hour 30 minutes **serves** 4
nutritional count per serving 22.9g total fat (10g saturated fat); 1756kJ (420 cal); 40.2g carbohydrate; 11.3g protein; 4.7g fibre

Sprinkle the combined cheese and breadcrumbs over potatoes.

layered potatoes

500g ruby lou potatoes, unpeeled
100g butter, melted
2 cloves garlic, crushed
¾ cup (60g) finely grated parmesan cheese
6 green onions, sliced thinly
½ cup coarsely chopped fresh flat-leaf parsley

1 Preheat oven to 200°C/180°C fan-forced. Line bases of four 1-cup (250ml) metal moulds or ovenproof baking dishes with baking paper.

2 Using sharp knife, mandoline or V-slicer, slice potatoes into 2mm slices; pat dry with absorbent paper. Place a few potato slices in each mould, dot with a little of the combined butter and garlic, cheese, onion and parsley. Continue layering remaining ingredients, finishing with potato; cover each mould with foil, place on oven tray. Bake in oven about 30 minutes or until potato is tender. Stand 5 minutes before turning out.

prep + cook time 1 hour **serves** 4
nutritional count per serving 25.6g total fat (16.6g saturated fat); 1421kJ (340 cal); 17.4g carbohydrate; 9.2g protein; 3.1g fibre

You can also use desiree or pontiac potatoes for this recipe.

scalloped potatoes

1.2kg desiree potatoes, peeled
150g leg ham, chopped finely
300ml pouring cream
¾ cup (180ml) milk
¾ cup (90g) coarsely grated cheddar cheese

1 Preheat oven to 180°C/160°C fan-forced; oil 1.5-litre (6-cup) baking dish.
2 Using sharp knife, mandoline or V-slicer, slice potatoes into 2mm slices; pat dry with absorbent paper. Layer a quarter of the potato in dish; top with a third of the ham. Continue layering remaining potato and ham, finishing with potato.
3 Heat cream and milk in small saucepan until almost boiling; pour over potato mixture. Cover with foil; bake in oven 30 minutes. Remove foil; bake 20 minutes. Top with cheese; bake, uncovered, about 20 minutes or until potato is tender. Stand 10 minutes before serving.

prep + cook time 1 hour 30 minutes **serves** 6
nutritional count per serving 29.5g total fat (18.8g saturated fat); 1864kJ (446 cal); 29.1g carbohydrate; 15.2g protein; 3.2g fibre

This scrumptious layered dish of potato, ham, cream and cheese is certain to become one of your family's favourites. You can also use coliban or sebago potatoes for this recipe.

potatoes byron

1kg russet burbank potatoes, unpeeled
60g butter, chopped
½ cup (125ml) pouring cream
¼ cup (20g) finely grated parmesan cheese
¼ cup (30g) finely grated gruyère cheese

1 Preheat oven to 180°C/160°C fan-forced. Oil four shallow 1-cup (250ml) ovenproof dishes.
2 Pierce skin of each potato with fork; place on oven tray. Bake, uncovered, about 1 hour or until tender. Cover; cool 10 minutes.
3 Split potatoes in half lengthways; scoop flesh into medium bowl, discard potato skins. Mash potato with butter.
4 Lightly divide potato among prepared dishes. Pour cream evenly over potato; sprinkle with combined cheeses. Bake, uncovered, in oven, about 10 minutes or until heated through and browned lightly.

prep + cook time 1 hour 20 minutes **serves** 4
nutritional count per serving 30.2g total fat (19.7g saturated fat); 1910kJ (457 cal); 33.8g carbohydrate; 10.8g protein; 5g fibre

You can also use pink-eye or sebago potatoes for this recipe.

portuguese potatoes

600g sebago potatoes, peeled, chopped coarsely
2 tablespoons olive oil
2 cloves garlic, crushed
1 large brown onion (200g), chopped coarsely
4 medium tomatoes (760g), chopped coarsely
2 teaspoons sweet paprika
2 teaspoons finely chopped fresh thyme
½ cup (125ml) chicken stock
1 tablespoon peri-peri sauce
1 tablespoon coarsely chopped fresh flat-leaf parsley

1 Preheat oven to 220°C/200°C fan-forced.
2 Toss potato and half the oil in medium shallow baking dish. Roast, uncovered, about 30 minutes or until browned lightly.
3 Meanwhile, heat remaining oil in large frying pan; cook garlic and onion, stirring, until onion softens. Add tomato, paprika and thyme to pan; cook, stirring, about 1 minute or until tomato just softens. Add stock and sauce to pan; bring to the boil. Reduce heat; simmer, uncovered, stirring occasionally, about 10 minutes or until sauce thickens slightly.
4 Remove potato from oven; reduce oven temperature to 180°C/160°C fan-forced.
5 Pour sauce over potato; bake, uncovered, about 20 minutes or until potato is tender. Serve sprinkled with parsley.

prep + cook time 1 hour 10 minutes **serves** 6
nutritional count per serving 6.5g total fat (0.9g saturated fat); 656kJ (157 cal); 18.2g carbohydrate; 4.5g protein; 3.9g fibre

Peri-peri (piri-piri) is a hot Portuguese sauce made of chilli, garlic, ginger, oil and herbs, and is available from supermarkets. You can also use pontiac potatoes for this recipe.

baked potatoes

The perfect baked potato should be salty on the outside and snow white and fluffy on the inside. You can also use russet burbank or spunta potatoes for this recipe.

8 king edward potatoes (1.4kg), unpeeled

1 Preheat oven to 180°C/160°C fan-forced.
2 Pierce skin of each potato with a skewer or fork; wrap each potato in foil, place on oven tray. Bake about 1 hour or until tender. Top with one of the topping on page 77.

prep + cook time 1 hour 10 minutes makes 8
nutritional count per potato 0.2g total fat (0g saturated fat); 493kJ (118 cal); 22.9g carbohydrate; 4.2g protein; 3.5g fibre

Pierce the skin of each potato to prevent it from splitting while in the oven.

Wrapping the potatoes completely in foil results in a soft skin after baking.

toppings

prep + cook time 5 minutes

Each of these toppings is enough for eight potatoes.

lime and chilli yogurt

Combine ⅔ cup yogurt, 2 tablespoons chopped fresh coriander, 2 fresh small finely chopped red thai chillies and 1 teaspoon finely grated lime rind in small bowl; refrigerate until required.

nutritional count per potato 1g total fat (0.5g saturated fat); 564kJ (135 cal); 24.1g carbohydrate; 5.3g protein; 3.5g fibre

cream cheese and pesto

Combine ⅔ cup spreadable cream cheese, ½ teaspoon cracked black pepper and ⅓ cup pesto in small bowl; refrigerate until required.

nutritional count per potato 11.3g total fat (5.2g saturated fat); 966kJ (231 cal); 23.6g carbohydrate; 7g protein; 3.8g fibre

mustard and walnut butter

Mash 60g softened butter, 1 teaspoon wholegrain mustard and 2 tablespoons finely chopped roasted walnuts in small bowl until mixture forms a paste; refrigerate until required.

nutritional count per potato 7.9g total fat (4.1g saturated fat); 790kJ (189 cal); 23.1g carbohydrate; 4.6g protein; 3.7g fibre

A lightly oiled potato rolled in sea salt will result in a crisp crunchy skin.

From top: cream cheese and pesto; lime and chilli yogurt; mustard and walnut butter.

fennel and potato gratin

800g sebago potatoes, peeled
2 small fennel bulbs (400g), sliced thinly
1 tablespoon plain flour
1¾ cups (430ml) pouring cream
¼ cup (60ml) milk
20g butter, chopped
¾ cup (90g) coarsely grated cheddar cheese
¾ cup (50g) stale breadcrumbs

1 Preheat oven to 180°C/160°C fan-forced; oil deep 2-litre (8-cup) baking dish.
2 Using sharp knife, mandoline or V-slicer, slice potatoes into 2mm slices; pat dry with absorbent paper. Layer a quarter of the potato slices into baking dish; top with a third of the fennel. Continue layering remaining potato and fennel, finishing with potato.
3 Blend flour with a little of the cream in medium jug to form a smooth paste; stir in remaining cream and milk. Pour cream mixture over potato; dot with butter. Cover with foil; bake in oven about 1 hour or until vegetables are just tender. Remove foil, top with combined cheese and breadcrumbs; bake, uncovered, about 15 minutes or until top is browned lightly.

prep + cook time 1 hour 35 minutes **serves** 8
nutritional count per serving 29.7g total fat (19.4g saturated fat); 1634kJ (391 cal); 21.7g carbohydrate; 8.1g protein; 3.4g fibre

A gratin is any recipe that uses a topping of breadcrumbs, cheese and small pieces of butter, which is then heated under a grill or in an oven until browned and crisp. You can also use spunta potatoes for this recipe.

creamed potatoes with rosemary and cheese

1kg spunta potatoes, peeled
300ml pouring cream
2 cloves garlic, crushed
2 chicken stock cubes, crumbled
¼ teaspoon cracked black pepper
1 tablespoon finely chopped fresh rosemary
½ cup (40g) finely grated parmesan cheese

1 Preheat oven to 180°C/160°C fan-forced; oil shallow 2.5-litre (10-cup) ovenproof dish.
2 Using sharp knife, mandoline or V-slicer, slice potatoes into 2mm slices; pat dry with absorbent paper. Combine cream, garlic, stock cubes, pepper and rosemary in small bowl.
3 Layer a quarter of the potato slices, slightly overlapping, in dish; top with a quarter of the cream mixture. Continue layering remaining potato and cream mixture.
4 Press potato firmly with spatula to completely submerge in cream, cover with foil; bake in oven 1 hour. Remove foil; sprinkle with cheese. Bake, uncovered, about 20 minutes or until potato is tender and cheese browns lightly. Stand 10 minutes before serving.

prep + cook time 1 hour 35 minutes **serves** 6
nutritional count per serving 24.1g total fat (15.7g saturated fat); 1446kJ (346 cal); 23.7g carbohydrate; 7.7g protein; 2.8g fibre

You can also use desiree or russet burbank potatoes for this recipe.

tiella

2 small eggplants (460g)
2 tablespoons coarse cooking salt
1kg medium tomatoes, peeled, seeded, chopped finely
1 medium brown onion (150g), chopped finely
2 stalks celery (300g), trimmed, chopped finely
2 cloves garlic, crushed
1 tablespoon finely chopped fresh oregano
1 tablespoon finely chopped fresh flat-leaf parsley
1kg sebago potatoes, peeled
¼ cup (60ml) olive oil
2 tablespoons fresh oregano leaves

1 Cut eggplants into thin slices, sprinkle with salt; stand in colander in sink 30 minutes. Rinse eggplant well under cold water; pat dry with absorbent paper.
2 Preheat oven to 180°C/160°C fan-forced.
3 Combine tomato, onion, celery, garlic, chopped oregano and parsley in medium bowl.
4 Using sharp knife, mandoline or V-slicer, slice potatoes into 2mm slices; pat dry with absorbent paper. Place half the potato in lightly oiled shallow 3-litre (12-cup) baking dish; top with half the eggplant, half the tomato mixture, then drizzle with half the oil. Repeat layering with potato, eggplant, tomato mixture and oil.
5 Cover dish with foil; bake in oven 1 hour. Remove foil; bake in oven about 30 minutes or until vegetables are tender. Sprinkle tiella with oregano leaves.

prep + cook time 2 hours 10 minutes (+ standing)
serves 8
nutritional count per serving 7.2g total fat (1g saturated fat); 723kJ (173 cal); 20.1g carbohydrate; 4.6g protein; 4.6g fibre

Originating in southern Italy, tiella is a traditional Calabrian layered vegetable casserole; it is also the name of the earthenware cooking pot the dish is cooked in.

mashes, smashes and creams

the perfect mash

For the most lusciously smooth, fluffy, irresistible mash, this is the recipe to follow. Use potatoes that are high in starch and take care not to overcook them. Push the potato through a sieve, as we suggest here, or through a potato ricer or food mill (mouli). You can also use pink-eye or sebago potatoes for this recipe.

1kg lasoda potatoes, peeled, cut into 3cm pieces
40g butter, softened
¾ cup (180ml) hot milk

1 Place potato in medium saucepan with enough cold water to barely cover the potato. Boil, uncovered, over medium heat about 15 minutes or until potato is tender. Drain.

2 Using the back of a wooden spoon, push potato through fine sieve into large bowl. Use spoon to stir butter and hot milk into potato, folding gently until mash is smooth and fluffy.

prep + cook time 30 minutes serves 4
nutritional count per serving 10.2g total fat (6.6g saturated fat); 1133kJ (271 cal); 35g carbohydrate; 7.6g protein; 4g fibre

tips Mash the potato in a bowl with a traditional potato masher. Don't try to mash potato in a food processor as it will become gluey. After potato is drained, work quickly, never allowing it to become cold. Heat any liquid ingredients you intend to stir into the mash.
Different potato varieties absorb different amounts of water when cooked, and the method of cooking (steaming, microwaving or boiling) also determines how much water is absorbed into the cooked potato. The age of the potato also has an effect on the amount of liquid it can absorb, therefore, the amount of liquid needed for a perfect mash will vary. With practice, you should be able to tell by looking at a mash mixture when it has had the right amount of liquid added. We found that lasoda potatoes gave the smoothest and most delicious mash.

Use a wooden spoon to push the potato through a fine sieve.

A potato ricer is great when making small amounts of mash.

A food mill (mouli) will also ensure the mash is lump-free.

cottage pie

1 tablespoon olive oil
2 cloves garlic, crushed
1 large brown onion (200g), chopped finely
2 medium carrots (240g), peeled, chopped finely
1kg beef mince
1 tablespoon worcestershire sauce
2 tablespoons tomato paste
2 x 425g cans crushed tomatoes
1 teaspoon dried mixed herbs
200g button mushrooms, quartered
1 cup (120g) frozen peas
1kg sebago potatoes, peeled, chopped coarsely
¾ cup (180ml) hot milk
40g butter, softened
½ cup (50g) coarsely grated pizza cheese

1 Heat oil in large saucepan; cook garlic, onion and carrot, stirring, until onion softens. Add beef; cook, stirring, about 10 minutes or until changed in colour.
2 Add sauce, paste, undrained tomatoes and herbs to pan; bring to the boil. Reduce heat; simmer, uncovered, about 30 minutes or until mixture thickens slightly. Stir in mushrooms and peas.
3 Preheat oven to 180°C/160°C fan-forced.
4 Meanwhile, boil, steam or microwave potato until tender; drain. Mash potato in large bowl with milk and butter.
5 Pour beef mixture into deep 3-litre (12-cup) ovenproof dish; top with mashed potato mixture, sprinkle with cheese. Bake, uncovered, in oven about 35 minutes or until pie is heated through and top is browned lightly.

prep + cook time 2 hours **serves** 8
nutritional count per serving 20.7g total fat (9.5g saturated fat); 1806kJ (432 cal); 26.3g carbohydrate; 32.2g protein; 6.2g fibre

tips You can make the cottage pie up to two days in advance; keep, covered, in the refrigerator. Reheat, covered, in 160°C/140°C fan-forced oven for about 40 minutes. The pie can also be frozen for up to three months; thaw overnight in the refrigerator before reheating as above.

basic mash with flavours from the pantry

1kg lasoda potatoes, peeled, chopped coarsely
50g butter, softened
½ cup (125ml) hot pouring cream

flavour variations

- 4 cloves mashed roasted garlic
- 340g can asparagus, drained, chopped finely, combined with ¾ cup grated parmesan cheese
- 310g can creamed corn
- 2 teaspoons wasabi paste
- 1 tablespoon sun-dried tomato pesto
- 2 tablespoons basil pesto
- 180g can tuna chunks in springwater, drained, flaked
- 2 teaspoons sambal oelek
- ½ cup (150g) bottled apple sauce

1 Boil, steam or microwave potato until tender; drain.

2 Meanwhile, prepare your choice of flavour variation.

3 Mash potato, butter and cream in large bowl until smooth; stir in your flavour variation.

prep + cook time 30 minutes, depending on the flavour variation.
serves 4
nutritional count per serving (without flavour variation) 24.5g total fat (15.8g saturated fat); 1893kJ (452 cal); 46.6g carbohydrate; 8.2g protein; 6.6g fibre

tips See page 85 for tips on how to make the perfect mashed potato. If necessary, prepare flavour variation before cooking potato.

gnocchi

Gnocchi should be light, delicate, pillow-like dumplings that virtually melt on the tongue – it's very addictive when made properly. We provide you with three different serving sauces (see pages 92-93), but most of your favourite pasta sauces will suit gnocchi just as well. Each of the sauce recipes makes enough to accompany this gnocchi recipe.

1kg russet burbank potatoes, unpeeled
2 eggs, beaten lightly
30g butter, melted
¼ cup (20g) finely grated parmesan cheese
2 cups (300g) plain flour, approximately

Add enough of the flour to the mixture to make a firm dough.

Use fingers to roll one part of dough into 2cm-thick sausage shape.

1 Boil or steam whole potatoes until tender; drain. Peel when cool enough to handle. Mash, using ricer, food mill (mouli), or sieve and a wooden spoon, into large bowl; stir in eggs, butter, cheese and enough of the flour to make a firm dough.
2 Divide dough into eight equal portions; roll each portion on lightly floured surface into 2cm-thick sausage-shape. Cut each sausage-shape into 2cm pieces; roll pieces into balls.
3 Roll each ball along the tines of a fork, pressing lightly on top of ball with index finger to form classic gnocchi shape, grooved on one side and dimpled on the other. Place gnocchi, in single layer, on lightly floured tray, cover; refrigerate 1 hour.
4 Cook gnocchi in large saucepan of boiling salted water about 3 minutes or until gnocchi float to the surface. Remove from pan with slotted spoon; drain. Serve hot, with the sauce of your choice.

prep + cook time 1 hour (+ refrigeration) **serves** 8
nutritional count per serving 5.8g total fat (3g saturated fat); 1145kJ (274 cal); 43.4g carbohydrate; 9.7g protein; 3.9g fibre

tips Add 1 teaspoon of any finely chopped herb you wish, such as rosemary, thyme, sage or oregano, to the gnocchi dough.
Potato should be mashed while hot, but it can be cooled slightly before being mixed with remaining ingredients.

Roll each ball along the tines of a fork to form gnocchi shape.

Each of these sauce recipes makes enough to accompany the gnocchi recipe on page 90.

three-cheese sauce

60g butter
⅓ cup (50g) plain flour
2 cups (500ml) milk
300ml pouring cream
60g coarsely grated provolone cheese
70g coarsely grated fontina cheese
40g gorgonzola cheese, crumbled

1 Melt butter in medium saucepan. Add flour; cook, stirring, until mixture thickens and bubbles. Gradually add milk and cream; stir until mixture boils and thickens. Remove from heat; stir in cheeses.

prep + cook time 15 minutes serves 8
nutritional count per serving (without gnocchi) 31.6 total fat (20.1g saturated fat); 1467kJ (351 cal); 8.6g carbohydrate; 8.9g protein; 0.2g fibre

tip Sprinkle over chopped flat-leaf parsely, to serve.

tomato sauce

2 tablespoons olive oil
1 large brown onion (200g), chopped finely
2 cloves garlic, crushed
2 tablespoons tomato paste
2 x 425g cans crushed tomatoes
¼ cup finely shredded fresh basil leaves

1 Heat oil in medium heavy-based saucepan; cook onion and garlic, stirring, until onion softens.
2 Add tomato paste; cook, stirring, 1 minute. Stir in undrained tomatoes; bring to the boil. Reduce heat; simmer, uncovered, about 30 minutes or until sauce thickens slightly. Stir in basil.

prep + cook time 45 minutes serves 8
nutritional count per serving (without gnocchi) 4.8g total fat (0.6g saturated fat); 309kJ (74 cal); 5.3g carbohydrate; 1.4g protein; 2g fibre

tip Sprinkle over grated parmesan cheese, to serve.

classic pesto

2 cloves garlic, quartered
¼ cup (40g) roasted pine nuts
¼ cup (20g) finely grated parmesan cheese
1 cup firmly packed fresh basil leaves
⅓ cup (80ml) olive oil
½ cup (125ml) pouring cream

1 Blend or process garlic, nuts, cheese and basil until finely chopped. With motor operating, gradually add oil in a thin steady stream; process until pesto is thick.
2 Just before serving, transfer pesto to small saucepan, add cream; stir over low heat until heated through.

prep + cook time 15 minutes serves 8
nutritional count per serving (without gnocchi) 20.2g total fat (6.5g saturated fat); 376kJ (190 cal); 0.7g carbohydrate; 1.9g protein; 0.4g fibre

potato crush

1kg baby new potatoes, unpeeled
½ cup (120g) sour cream
40g butter, softened

1 Boil, steam or microwave whole potatoes until tender; drain.
2 Mash about half the unpeeled whole potatoes, sour cream and butter in large bowl until smooth; stir in one of the flavour variations (see page 95).
3 Using back of a fork or potato masher, gently crush remaining potatoes until skins burst and flesh is just flattened; fold into mash mixture.

prep + cook time 20 minutes, depending on the flavour variation.
serves 4
nutritional count per serving 20.4g total fat (13.2g saturated fat); 1480kJ (354 cal); 33.7g carbohydrate; 6.8g protein; 5g fibre

Mash half of the potatoes with the sour cream and butter in a large bowl.

Once the potato mash is smooth, stir in one of the flavour variations.

original potato salad

Combine 6 coarsely chopped drained cornichons, 3 coarsely chopped green onions, ¼ cup coarsely chopped fresh flat-leaf parsley and 1 tablespoon coarsely chopped rinsed drained capers in bowl.

nutritional count per serving (including potato crush) 20.5g total fat (13.2g saturated fat); 1547kJ (370 cal); 37.5g carbohydrate; 6.7g protein; 5g fibre

caesar salad

Fry 3 finely chopped bacon slices in oiled frying pan until crisp; drain on absorbent paper. Combine with 4 finely chopped anchovies, 1 crushed garlic clove, 3 thinly sliced green onions and ½ cup shaved parmesan cheese in bowl.

nutritional count per serving (including potato crush) 25.8g total fat (16.1g saturated fat); 1873kJ (448 cal); 34.5g carbohydrate; 17.7g protein; 4.5g fibre

herb and mustard salad

Combine 1 tablespoon wholegrain mustard, ¼ cup coarsely chopped fresh chives, ¼ cup coarsely chopped fresh flat-leaf parsley, 2 tablespoons coarsely chopped fresh basil and 2 tablespoons coarsely chopped fresh dill in bowl.

nutritional count per serving (including potato crush) 20.5g total fat (13.2g saturated fat); 1480kJ (354 cal); 33.5g carbohydrate; 6.5g protein; 4.7g fibre

Gently crush the remaining potatoes until skins burst and flesh is just flattened.

kipfler crush

1kg kipfler potatoes, unpeeled
40g butter, softened
½ cup (120g) sour cream
½ cup (125ml) hot milk

1 Boil, steam or microwave unpeeled potatoes until tender; drain.
2 Mash about half the unpeeled whole potatoes with butter, sour cream and milk in large bowl until smooth; stir in one of the flavour variations (see page 95), if desired.
3 Using back of a fork or potato masher, gently crush remaining potatoes until skins burst and flesh is just flattened; fold into mash mixture.

prep + cook time 30 minutes serves 4
nutritional count per serving 21.6g total fat (14g saturated fat); 1568kJ (375 cal); 35.2g carbohydrate; 7.8g protein; 5g fibre

mashed potato casserole

500g sebago potatoes, peeled, chopped coarsely
30g butter, softened
2 eggs, beaten lightly
300ml pouring cream
1 cup (120g) coarsely grated cheddar cheese
2 tablespoons coarsely chopped fresh chives

1 Boil, steam or microwave potato until tender; drain. Mash potato in large bowl with butter until smooth; spread over base of lightly oiled shallow 1.5-litre (6-cup) baking dish.

2 Preheat oven to 180°C/160°C fan-forced.

3 Combine remaining ingredients in medium bowl; pour over potato. Bake, uncovered, about 40 minutes or until top sets and is browned.

prep + cook time 1 hour 10 minutes **serves** 4
nutritional count per serving 51.5g total fat (32.7g saturated fat); 2495kJ (597 cal); 18.7g carbohydrate; 15.4g protein; 2g fibre

To make individual dishes, divide mixture among four 1½-cup (375ml) ovenproof dishes. Cooking time will be 30 minutes. You can also use coliban or nicola potatoes for this recipe.

potato and vegetable mashes

Each of these mashes is enough to serve 4 people as a side dish.

broad bean mash

Shell 1kg fresh broad beans, discard pods. Boil, steam or microwave beans until just tender; drain. Peel away grey-coloured outer shells; blend or process beans until smooth. Stir in 2 tablespoons hot pouring cream. Boil, steam or microwave 1kg peeled, coarsely chopped lasoda potato until tender; drain. Mash potato in large bowl; stir in mashed bean mixture, 40g melted butter and another 2 tablespoons hot pouring cream.

prep + cook time 30 minutes **serves** 4
nutritional count per serving 17.9g total fat (11.3g saturated fat); 1810kJ (433 cal); 44.3g carbohydrate; 18.1g protein; 11.1g fibre

capsicum mash

Quarter 2 medium red capsicums; discard seeds and membranes. Roast under hot grill, skin-side up, until skin blisters and blackens. Cover capsicum pieces with plastic or paper for 5 minutes, then peel away skin; chop capsicum coarsely. Blend or process capsicum until smooth. Meanwhile, boil, steam or microwave 1kg peeled, coarsely chopped lasoda potato until tender; drain. Mash potato in large bowl; stir in ½ cup hot pouring cream and 20g softened butter. Add capsicum to mash; stir until combined.

prep + cook time 30 minutes **serves** 4
nutritional count per serving 18g total fat (11.6g saturated fat); 1446kJ (346 cal); 36.2g carbohydrate; 7.7g protein; 4.7g fibre

kumara mash

Boil, steam or microwave 500g peeled, coarsely chopped lasoda potato and 500g peeled, coarsely chopped kumara, together, until tender; drain. Mash potato and kumara in large bowl; stir in ¼ cup hot chicken stock and 40g melted butter.

prep + cook time 30 minutes **serves** 4
nutritional count per serving 8.5g total fat (5.4g saturated fat); 1024kJ (245 cal); 34.2g carbohydrate; 5.6g protein; 4.3g fibre

fennel mash

Slice 1 large fennel bulb thinly. Melt 60g butter in large frying pan; cook fennel, covered, over low heat, about 10 minutes or until fennel is very soft. Blend or process fennel until smooth. Meanwhile, boil, steam or microwave 1kg peeled, coarsely chopped lasoda potato until tender; drain. Mash potato in large bowl; stir in fennel mixture and ½ cup hot pouring cream.

prep + cook time 30 minutes **serves** 4
nutritional count per serving 13.8g total fat (8.9g saturated fat); 1296kJ (310 cal); 36g carbohydrate; 7.3g protein; 6.1g fibre

potato and vegetable mashes

spinach mash

Boil, steam or microwave 1kg peeled, coarsely chopped lasoda potato until tender; drain. Meanwhile, boil, steam or microwave 220g spinach leaves until wilted; drain. Squeeze out excess liquid. Blend or process spinach with 40g softened butter until almost smooth. Mash potato in large bowl; stir in ½ cup hot pouring cream and spinach mixture.

prep + cook time 30 minutes **serves** 4
nutritional count per serving 22.1g total fat (14.3g saturated fat); 1576kJ (377 cal); 34g carbohydrate; 8g protein; 5.5g fibre

pea mash

Boil, steam or microwave 1kg peeled, coarsely chopped lasoda potato and 1½ cups frozen peas, separately, until tender; drain. Mash potato in large bowl; stir in ¾ cup hot milk and 50g softened butter. Using fork, mash peas in small bowl; stir into potato mixture.

prep + cook time 30 minutes **serves** 4
nutritional count per serving 12.6g total fat (8g saturated fat); 1392kJ (333 cal); 39.8g carbohydrate; 11.1g protein; 7.5g fibre

celeriac mash

Boil, steam or microwave 800g peeled, coarsely chopped lasoda potato and 1kg peeled, coarsely chopped celeriac, separately, until tender; drain. Mash potato and celeriac in large bowl; stir in ½ cup hot pouring cream and 60g softened butter.

prep + cook time 30 minutes **serves** 4
nutritional count per serving 26.5g total fat (17g saturated fat); 1835kJ (439 cal); 39.7g carbohydrate; 5.5g protein; 10.7g fibre

pumpkin mash

Boil, steam or microwave 500g peeled, coarsely chopped lasoda potato and 500g peeled, coarsely chopped pumpkin together until tender; drain. Mash potato and pumpkin in large bowl; stir in 30g softened butter.

prep + cook time 30 minutes **serves** 4
nutritional count per serving 6.8g total fat (4.4g saturated fat); 790kJ (189 cal); 24.4g carbohydrate; 5.7g protein; 3.5g fibre

smoked fish pot pies

750g smoked cod fillets
2 cups (500ml) milk
1 bay leaf
6 black peppercorns
1kg coliban potatoes, peeled, chopped coarsely
50g butter, softened
20g butter, extra
1 large brown onion (200g), chopped finely
1 clove garlic, crushed
¼ cup (35g) plain flour
2½ cups (625ml) milk, extra
1 cup (120g) frozen peas
1 teaspoon finely grated lemon rind
2 tablespoons lemon juice
2 hard-boiled eggs, quartered

1 Place fish, milk, bay leaf and peppercorns in medium saucepan; bring to the boil. Reduce heat; simmer, uncovered, 10 minutes. Drain; discard liquid and spices. Remove and discard skin from fish; flake flesh into large chunks in medium bowl.
2 Meanwhile, boil, steam or microwave potato until tender; drain. Mash potato with softened butter in large bowl; cover to keep warm.
3 Melt extra butter in medium saucepan; cook onion and garlic, stirring, until onion softens. Add flour; cook, stirring, until mixture thickens and bubbles. Gradually add extra milk; stir until mixture boils and thickens. Add peas, rind and juice; remove from heat. Stir in fish.
4 Divide egg, fish mixture and potato mixture among four 2-cup (500ml) flameproof dishes. Place dishes on oven tray under very hot grill until tops are browned lightly.

prep + cook time 1 hour **serves** 4
nutritional count per serving 30.4g total fat (18.1g saturated fat); 3160kJ (756 cal); 58.8g carbohydrate; 57.7g protein; 6.8g fibre

You can also use lasoda or nicola potatoes for this recipe.

baked creamed potatoes

1kg lasoda potatoes, peeled, chopped coarsely
20g butter
3 rindless bacon slices (195g), chopped finely
4 green onions, chopped finely
½ cup (150g) mayonnaise
½ cup (120g) sour cream
½ cup (125ml) pouring cream
2 eggs, beaten lightly
1 tablespoon wholegrain mustard
¼ cup coarsely chopped fresh flat-leaf parsley
¾ cup (60g) finely grated parmesan cheese

1 Boil, steam or microwave potato until tender; drain.
2 Meanwhile, melt butter in medium frying pan; cook bacon and onion, stirring, until bacon is crisp.
3 Preheat oven to 180°C/160°C fan-forced.
4 Mash potato in large bowl with mayonnaise, sour cream and cream until smooth. Stir bacon mixture, eggs, mustard, parsley and ⅔ of the cheese into potato mixture. Spread mixture into lightly oiled shallow 1.75-litre (7-cup) baking dish; sprinkle with remaining cheese. Bake, uncovered, about 30 minutes or until top browns and potato mixture just sets.

prep + cook time 1 hour 10 minutes **serves** 4
nutritional count per serving 54g total fat (26.5g saturated fat); 3227kJ (772 cal); 42.6g carbohydrate; 27.7g protein; 4.6g fibre

We used whole-egg mayonnaise. You can also use pink-eye or sebago potatoes for this recipe.

mash-filled cabbage rolls with cheesy cream sauce

1kg sebago potatoes, peeled, chopped coarsely
40g butter, softened
1 egg yolk
4 large cabbage leaves
4 rindless bacon slices (260g), chopped coarsely
¼ cup (30g) coarsely grated cheddar cheese

cheesy cream sauce
20g butter
¼ cup (35g) plain flour
1½ cups (375ml) chicken stock
½ cup (125ml) pouring cream
½ cup (60g) coarsely grated cheddar cheese
¼ cup finely chopped fresh flat-leaf parsley

1 Boil, steam or microwave potato until tender; drain. Mash potato in large bowl with butter and egg yolk.

2 Meanwhile, discard thick stems from cabbage. Boil, steam or microwave leaves until just pliable; drain. Rinse under cold water; drain. Pat dry with absorbent paper.

3 Preheat oven to 200°C/180°C fan-forced. Make cheesy cream sauce.

4 Place leaves, vein-side up, on board. Cut leaves in half lengthways; divide potato mixture evenly among leaf halves, placing mixture at stem end. Roll firmly, folding in sides to enclose filling.

5 Place cabbage rolls, seam-side down, in shallow lightly oiled 2-litre (8-cup) ovenproof dish; pour cheesy cream sauce over rolls, sprinkle with bacon and cheese. Bake, uncovered, in oven about 20 minutes or until bacon is crisp and cabbage rolls are heated through.

cheesy cream sauce
Melt butter in medium saucepan, add flour; cook, stirring, until mixture thickens and bubbles. Gradually add stock and cream; stir until mixture boils and thickens. Stir in cheese and parsley.

prep + cook time 1 hour **serves** 4
nutritional count per serving 41.8g total fat (24.8g saturated fat); 2805kJ (671 cal); 41.9g carbohydrate; 30g protein; 5.5g fibre

You can also use lasoda or pink-eye potatoes for this recipe.

colcannon

1kg sebago potatoes, peeled, chopped coarsely
⅓ cup (80ml) hot pouring cream
80g butter, softened
2 medium brown onions (300g), chopped finely
1 clove garlic, crushed
350g savoy cabbage, shredded finely

1 Boil, steam or microwave potato until tender; drain. Mash potato, cream and half the butter in medium bowl until mixture is smooth.
2 Melt remaining butter in large frying pan; cook onion and garlic, stirring, until onion softens. Add cabbage; cook, stirring, about 2 minutes or until cabbage just wilts. Gently fold potato mixture into cabbage mixture.

prep + cook time 35 minutes **serves** 4
nutritional count per serving 25.5g total fat (16.5g saturated fat); 1835kJ (439 cal); 39.9g carbohydrate; 8.9g protein; 8.3g fibre

A hearty but meatless cabbage and potato dish served on Halloween in Ireland, colcannon traditionally had buried within its content a gold ring, coin, thimble and button. The diner who discovered the ring was supposed to marry within the year, while the coin symbolised wealth; the thimble and button meant the people who found them would not marry.

skordalia

400g russet burbank potatoes, peeled, chopped coarsely
2 slices white bread
½ cup (60g) ground almonds
3 cloves garlic, crushed
2 tablespoons apple cider vinegar
⅓ cup (80ml) water
¼ cup (60ml) olive oil

1 Boil, steam or microwave potato until tender; drain. Mash potato in medium bowl.
2 Meanwhile, trim and discard crusts from bread. Soak bread in small bowl of cold water; drain. Squeeze out excess water.
3 Blend or process bread with ground almonds, garlic, vinegar and the water until mixture is smooth. With motor operating, gradually add oil in a thin steady stream, processing until mixture thickens slightly. Fold bread mixture into potato mash.

prep + cook time 30 minutes makes 2 cups
nutritional count per tablespoon 3.7g total fat (0.4g saturated fat); 217kJ (52 cal); 3.2g carbohydrate; 1.1g protein; 0.6g fibre

Skordalia is a tangy Greek sauce or dip made with pureed potatoes and breadcrumbs or ground nuts (or, as in this case, both). Skordalia can be served with almost any kind of dish – from grilled meats and poultry to fish and raw vegetables.

duchesse potatoes

1kg nicola potatoes, peeled, chopped coarsely
3 egg yolks
100g butter, melted

1 Preheat oven to 180°C/160°C fan-forced; oil and line two oven trays with baking paper.
2 Boil, steam or microwave potato until tender; drain. Mash potato in large bowl with egg yolks and butter.
3 Spoon potato mixture into large piping bag fitted with a 1cm-fluted tube; pipe potato into 3cm rosette-shaped swirls onto oven trays.
4 Bake, uncovered, in oven about 30 minutes or until browned lightly.

prep + cook time 1 hour **makes** 40
nutritional count per rosette 2.5g total fat (1.5g saturated fat); 167kJ (40 cal); 3.3g carbohydrate; 0.8g protein; 0.4g fibre

tips For a variation, stir ½ cup finely grated parmesan cheese into the potato with the egg yolks and butter. The potato can be piped up to 3 hours ahead; keep, covered, in the refrigerator.

You can also use coliban or lasoda potatoes for this recipe.

smoked salmon pie

1kg pink-eye potatoes, peeled, chopped coarsely
40g butter, softened
¼ cup (60g) sour cream
200g smoked salmon, chopped coarsely
2 eggs, separated
2 green onions, chopped finely

1 Preheat oven to 200°C/180°C fan-forced.
2 Boil, steam or microwave potato until tender; drain. Mash potato in large bowl with butter and sour cream. Stir in salmon, one of the egg yolks, egg whites and onion.
3 Spoon mixture into oiled deep 22cm-round ovenproof dish; smooth top with spatula, brush with remaining egg yolk. Bake, uncovered, in oven, about 25 minutes or until pie is heated through and browned lightly.

prep + cook time 45 minutes **serves** 6
nutritional count per serving 12.9g total fat (7g saturated fat); 1120kJ (268 cal); 22.4g carbohydrate; 14.2g protein; 2.7g fibre

You could also use a 22cm-round loose-based flan tin for this recipe. You can also use lasoda or sebago potatoes for this recipe.

stuffed portobello mushrooms

500g lasoda potatoes, peeled, chopped coarsely
¼ cup (60ml) hot pouring cream
20g butter, softened
8 large portobello mushrooms (400g)
30g butter, melted, extra
1 tablespoon olive oil
1 small brown onion (80g), chopped finely
2 cloves garlic, crushed
1 fresh small red thai chilli, chopped finely
1 cup (120g) coarsely grated cheddar cheese
¼ cup coarsely chopped fresh flat-leaf parsley
2 tablespoons finely chopped fresh chives
1 teaspoon fresh thyme leaves

1 Preheat oven to 180°C/160°C fan-forced.
2 Boil, steam or microwave potato until tender; drain. Mash potato in large bowl with cream and softened butter. Cover to keep warm.
3 Meanwhile, remove and reserve stems from mushrooms. Brush caps with extra butter; place, stem-side up, on oven tray. Bake, uncovered, in oven 5 minutes; cover to keep warm.
4 Chop reserved stems finely. Heat oil in medium frying pan; cook onion, garlic, chilli and mushroom stems, stirring, until onion softens. Add cheese, parsley, chives and thyme; stir until combined.
5 Combine onion mixture with potato mixture; spoon mixture into mushroom caps.
6 Place caps on oven tray under hot grill about 5 minutes or until browned lightly.

prep + cook time 40 minutes serves 4
nutritional count per serving 31g total fat (18.1g saturated fat); 1789kJ (428 cal); 18.5g carbohydrate; 15g protein; 5.1g fibre

tip The portobello mushroom is really just a larger version of the swiss brown or cremini mushroom. Dense and hearty, it is a great variety to choose when making stuffed mushrooms. You can use swiss browns here, but purchase the largest ones you can find.

vegetarian tarts

1kg lasoda potatoes, peeled, chopped coarsely
½ cup (125ml) hot vegetable stock
30g butter
2 cloves garlic, crushed
200g mushrooms, sliced thickly
2 tablespoons finely shredded fresh basil
2 green onions, chopped finely
⅔ cup (80g) coarsely grated cheddar cheese
3 sheets fillo pastry
30g butter, melted

1 Boil, steam or microwave potato until tender; drain. Mash potato in large bowl with stock.
2 Meanwhile, melt butter in small frying pan; cook garlic and mushroom, stirring, until mushroom softens. Stir mushroom mixture, basil, onion and half the cheese into potato mixture.
3 Preheat oven to 200°C/180°C fan-forced. Oil four 1-cup (250ml) metal pie dishes. Place a 2.5cm x 30cm strip of baking paper over base of each dish, extending 5cm over sides of dishes.
4 Stack fillo sheets; cut stack in half crossways. Brush between layers with melted butter, then cut stack into four squares. Line prepared dishes with squares. Spoon potato mixture into dishes; sprinkle with remaining cheese.
5 Place dishes on oven tray; bake tarts in oven about 15 minutes or until pastry is browned lightly. Use baking paper strips to lift tarts out of dishes.

prep + cook time 45 minutes serves 4
nutritional count per serving 19.9g total fat (12.5g saturated fat); 1697kJ (406 cal); 39.3g carbohydrate; 14.5g protein; 5.9g fibre

You can also use nicola or sebago potatoes for this recipe.

potato dumplings with burnt butter

1kg pink-eye potatoes, unpeeled
1 clove garlic, crushed
50g butter, softened
2 eggs, beaten lightly
⅔ cup (100g) plain flour
¼ cup (20g) finely grated parmesan cheese
2 cups (500ml) water
1 litre (4 cups) chicken stock
125g butter, chopped
¼ cup loosely packed fresh sage leaves
1 teaspoon lemon juice

1 Boil, steam or microwave potatoes until tender; drain. When cool enough to handle, peel potatoes. Mash in large bowl with garlic and softened butter. Mix in egg, flour and cheese, stirring, until mixture forms a soft dough.
2 Bring the water and stock to the boil in large saucepan. Reduce heat; cook rounded tablespoons of the dough, in batches, in simmering stock mixture about 4 minutes or until dumplings rise to the surface. Using slotted spoon, remove dumplings; divide dumplings among serving bowls.
3 Meanwhile, melt chopped butter in small frying pan; when butter just sizzles, cook sage until crisp, drain on absorbent paper. Reheat butter in same pan; stir over low heat until just browned. Remove from heat; stir in juice. Drizzle dumplings with burnt butter; top with crisp sage leaves.

prep + cook time 1 hour 15 minutes serves 4
nutritional count per serving 41.7g total fat (26g saturated fat); 2767kJ (662 cal); 53g carbohydrate; 17g protein; 5.1g fibre

tip Potato flour can be used in place of wheat flour for a gluten-free version; make sure to use a gluten-free chicken stock as well.

You can also use lasoda or sebago potatoes for this recipe.

special-occasion mash

1kg sebago potatoes, peeled, chopped coarsely
1 cup (250g) mascarpone cheese
1 cup (80g) finely grated parmesan cheese
⅔ cup (80g) finely grated mozzarella cheese
½ cup (125ml) hot milk

1 Boil, steam or microwave potato until tender; drain. Mash potato in large bowl with remaining ingredients.

prep + cook time 30 minutes **serves** 4
nutritional count per serving 48.1g total fat (31.3g saturated fat); 2763kJ (661 cal); 35.4g carbohydrate; 20.7g protein; 4g fibre

You can also use coliban or pink-eye potatoes for this recipe.

salads, soups, sides and snacks

the perfect potato salad

Crisp, low-starch potatoes, such as bintje, desiree, kipfler and sebago, make the best potato salad. Take care not to overcook them or they will break apart or crumble.

2kg sebago potatoes, peeled
2 tablespoons apple cider vinegar
8 green onions, sliced thinly
¼ cup finely chopped fresh flat-leaf parsley

mayonnaise
2 egg yolks
1 teaspoon dijon mustard
2 teaspoons lemon juice
1 cup (250ml) vegetable oil
2 tablespoons hot water, approximately

1 Cut potatoes into 1.5cm pieces. Place potato in large saucepan, barely cover with cold water; cover saucepan, bring to the boil. Reduce heat; simmer, uncovered, stirring occasionally, until just tender. Drain, spread potato on a tray; sprinkle with vinegar. Cool 10 minutes. Refrigerate, covered, until cold.

2 Meanwhile, make mayonnaise.

3 Place potato in large bowl with mayonnaise, onion and parsley; mix gently to combine.

mayonnaise
Blend or process egg yolks, mustard and juice until smooth. With motor operating, gradually add oil in a thin, steady stream; process until mixture thickens. Add as much of the hot water as required to thin mayonnaise.
makes 1 cup

prep + cook time 40 minutes (+ refrigeration)
serves 8
nutritional count per serving 30.4g total fat (4.1g saturated fat); 1843kJ (441 cal); 33.3g carbohydrate; 7g protein; 4.2g fibre

After peeling the potatoes, cut them into around 1.5cm pieces.

Drain potato pieces when they are just tender.

Spread potato pieces on a tray, then drizzle with cider vinegar.

spanish tortilla

800g russet burbank potatoes, peeled, sliced thinly
1 tablespoon olive oil
1 large brown onion (200g), sliced thinly
200g chorizo sausage, sliced thinly
6 eggs, beaten lightly
300ml pouring cream
4 green onions, sliced thickly
¼ cup (25g) coarsely grated mozzarella cheese
¼ cup (30g) coarsely grated cheddar cheese

1 Boil, steam or microwave potato until just tender; drain.
2 Meanwhile, heat oil in medium frying pan; cook brown onion, stirring, until softened. Add chorizo; cook, stirring, until crisp. Drain chorizo mixture on absorbent paper.
3 Whisk eggs in large bowl with cream, green onion and cheeses; stir in potato and chorizo mixture.
4 Pour mixture into heated lightly oiled medium frying pan; cook, covered, over low heat, about 10 minutes or until tortilla is just set. Carefully invert tortilla onto plate, then slide back into pan; cook, uncovered, about 5 minutes or until cooked through.

prep + cook time 45 minutes **serves** 4
nutritional count per serving 68.1g total fat (34.1g saturated fat); 3683kJ (881 cal); 32.6g carbohydrate; 32.7g protein; 4.1g fibre

You can also use bintje or pink fir apple potatoes for this recipe.

bubble and squeak

450g nadine potatoes, peeled, chopped coarsely
250g cabbage, chopped coarsely
4 rindless bacon slices (260g), chopped coarsely
1 medium brown onion (150g), chopped coarsely

1 Boil, steam or microwave potato and cabbage, separately, until just tender; drain. Mash potato in medium bowl until smooth.
2 Meanwhile, cook bacon in heated large frying pan, stirring, until crisp; drain on absorbent paper.
3 Cook onion in pan, stirring, until softened. Add potato, cabbage and bacon; stir to combine. Flatten mixture to form large cake-shape; cook, uncovered, until bottom of potato cake is just browned. Carefully invert onto plate, then slide back into frying pan; cook, uncovered, until browned on other side.

prep + cook time 40 minutes serves 4
nutritional count per serving 6.4g total fat (2.3g saturated fat); 903kJ (216 cal); 18.7g carbohydrate; 18.4g protein; 4.5g fibre

Originally an English dish made from the leftovers of a roast dinner, usually cabbage, potatoes and, if any remained, meat. Bubble and squeak's name is supposedly derived from the sounds the ingredients make while being tossed together in a frying pan. You can also use lasoda or sebago potatoes for this recipe.

stuffed potatoes

Depending on what you decide to put in them, stuffed potatoes can make a light and healthy snack. We've given you these suggestions (pages 128-131) to indulge in, but use your favourite stuffing ideas if you prefer.

blue-cheese stuffed potatoes

8 coliban potatoes (960g), unpeeled
80g firm blue-vein cheese, crumbled
125g packet cream cheese
½ cup (150g) mayonnaise
½ cup (120g) sour cream
1 clove garlic, quartered
⅓ cup (40g) coarsely chopped roasted pecans
2 teaspoons finely chopped fresh chives

If microwaving raw potatoes, pierce the skin of each with a fork to prevent it splitting.

Using a sharp knife, cut a shallow slice from the top of each cooked potato.

1 Preheat oven to 200°C/180°C fan-forced. Lightly oil oven tray.

2 Boil, steam or microwave potatoes until just tender; drain.

3 Meanwhile, blend or process cheeses, mayonnaise, sour cream and garlic.

4 Cut a shallow slice from the top of each potato; using teaspoon, scoop flesh from each top into medium bowl, discard skin. Using teaspoon, carefully scoop about two-thirds of the flesh from each potato into same bowl; reserve potato shells.

5 Mash potato until smooth; stir in cheese mixture and half of the nuts. Place potato shells on prepared tray. Divide mixture among potato shells; bake, uncovered, in oven about 15 minutes or until heated through. Top with remaining nuts and chives.

prep + cook time 40 minutes **serves** 4

nutritional count per serving 36.3g total fat (12.7g saturated fat); 2299kJ (550 cal); 40g carbohydrate; 13.8g protein; 6g fibre

Using a teaspoon, carefully scoop out about two-thirds of the potato flesh.

chorizo stuffed potatoes

8 coliban potatoes (960g), unpeeled
1 teaspoon olive oil
70g chorizo sausage, chopped finely
1 clove garlic, crushed
1 cup (250g) canned crushed tomatoes
⅓ cup (90g) sour cream
2 tablespoons pizza cheese

1 Preheat oven to 200°C/180°C fan-forced. Lightly oil oven tray.
2 Boil, steam or microwave potatoes until tender; drain.
3 Meanwhile, heat oil in small frying pan; cook chorizo, stirring, about 3 minutes or until crisp. Drain on absorbent paper. Cook garlic in same pan, stirring over low heat, until just fragrant. Return chorizo to pan with undrained tomatoes; simmer, uncovered, until mixture reduces by half.
4 Cut shallow slice from top of each potato; using teaspoon, scoop flesh from each top into medium bowl, discard skin. Using teaspoon, carefully scoop about two-thirds of the flesh from each potato into same bowl; reserve potato shells.
5 Mash potato until smooth; stir in chorizo mixture and sour cream. Place potato shells on prepared tray. Divide mixture among potato shells, sprinkle with cheese; bake, uncovered, in oven about 15 minutes or until heated through.

prep + cook time 45 minutes **serves** 4
nutritional count per serving 17.1g total fat (8.5g saturated fat); 1459kJ (349 cal); 34.4g carbohydrate; 11g protein; 5.7g fibre

creamed corn stuffed potatoes

8 coliban potatoes (960g), unpeeled
1 teaspoon vegetable oil
30g sliced prosciutto, chopped coarsely
125g can creamed corn
2 tablespoons finely chopped fresh coriander

1 Preheat oven to 200°C/180°C fan-forced. Lightly oil oven tray.

2 Boil, steam or microwave potatoes until just tender; drain.

3 Meanwhile, heat oil in small frying pan; cook prosciutto, stirring, about 2 minutes or until crisp.

4 Cut shallow slice from top of each potato; using teaspoon, scoop flesh from each top into medium bowl, discard skin. Using teaspoon, carefully scoop about two-thirds of the flesh from each potato into same bowl; reserve potato shells.

5 Mash potato until smooth; stir in prosciutto, corn and coriander. Place potato shells on prepared tray. Divide mixture among potato shells; bake, uncovered, in oven, about 15 minutes or until heated through.

prep + cook time 45 minutes serves 4
nutritional count per serving 2g total fat (0.3g saturated fat); 878kJ (210 cal); 36.7g carbohydrate; 7.8g protein; 5.9g fibre

aloo gobi

450g ruby lou potatoes, peeled, chopped coarsely
1 tablespoon (20g) ghee
1 tablespoon black mustard seeds
1 tablespoon cumin seeds
3 cloves garlic, crushed
½ teaspoon ground turmeric
½ teaspoon garam masala
1 large brown onion (200g), sliced thinly
2 medium tomatoes (380g), chopped coarsely
1kg cauliflower, chopped coarsely
1 cup (250ml) water
¼ cup loosely packed fresh coriander leaves

1 Boil, steam or microwave potato until just tender; drain.

2 Meanwhile, melt ghee in large saucepan; cook seeds, stirring, until they begin to pop. Add garlic, turmeric and garam masala; cook, stirring, until mixture is fragrant. Add onion; cook, stirring, until onion softens. Add tomato and cauliflower; cook, stirring, 1 minute.

3 Stir in the water; bring to the boil. Reduce heat; simmer, covered, 10 minutes. Stir in potato; simmer, covered, about 5 minutes or until vegetables are tender. Remove from heat; stir in coriander.

prep + cook time 45 minutes **serves** 4
nutritional count per serving 5.2g total fat (2.9g saturated fat); 849kJ (203 cal); 24.8g carbohydrate; 10.1g protein; 8.5g fibre

Aloo means potato and gobi, cauliflower, to an Indian cook, but this easy-to-make dry curry means delicious in anyone's vocabulary.

potato patties with vegetable ragoût

1kg coliban potatoes, peeled, chopped coarsely
1 teaspoon olive oil
1 small brown onion (80g), chopped finely
1 clove garlic, crushed
1 egg, beaten lightly
1 tablespoon coarsely chopped fresh flat-leaf parsley
50g butter
2 tablespoons olive oil, extra

vegetable ragoût

30g butter
1 tablespoon olive oil
1 clove garlic, crushed
1 small brown onion (80g), chopped coarsely
2 stalks celery (300g), trimmed, chopped coarsely
1 medium zucchini (120g), chopped coarsely
150g button mushrooms, quartered
¼ cup (60ml) dry white wine
1 cup (260g) bottled tomato pasta sauce
½ cup (125ml) vegetable stock
½ cup (75g) seeded kalamata olives
2 tablespoons coarsely chopped fresh flat-leaf parsley

1 Boil, steam or microwave potato until just tender; drain. Mash roughly in large bowl.
2 Meanwhile, heat oil in small frying pan; cook onion and garlic, stirring, until onion softens.
3 Add onion mixture to potato with egg and parsley; stir to combine. Refrigerate 1 hour.
4 Meanwhile, make vegetable ragoût.
5 Using floured hands, shape potato mixture into eight patties. Heat butter and extra oil in large frying pan; cook patties, in batches, until browned both sides. Serve patties with vegetable ragoût.

vegetable ragoût

Heat butter and oil in medium saucepan; cook garlic, onion and celery, stirring, until vegetables soften. Add zucchini and mushrooms; cook, stirring, 2 minutes. Add wine; cook, stirring, 1 minute. Add sauce, stock and olives; bring to the boil. Reduce heat; simmer, uncovered, about 10 minutes or until vegetables are cooked through. Remove from heat; stir in parsley.

prep + cook time 1 hour (+ refrigeration) **serves** 4
nutritional count per serving 53.2g total fat (21.5g saturated fat); 3026kJ (724 cal); 44g carbohydrate; 12g protein; 8.7g fibre

Ragoût, which comes from the French verb, ragoûter, meaning 'to stimulate the appetite', does exactly that in this dish. This mixture is quite soft to handle. You can also use lasoda or nicola potatoes for this recipe.

samosas

1½ cups (225g) plain flour
1 tablespoon ghee
1 tablespoon cumin seeds
½ cup (125ml) warm water, approximately
vegetable oil, for deep-frying

potato masala filling

125g coliban potatoes, peeled, chopped finely
1 teaspoon ghee
½ small brown onion (40g), chopped finely
1 clove garlic, crushed
½ fresh large green chilli, chopped finely
1 teaspoon grated fresh ginger
¼ teaspoon coriander seeds
¼ teaspoon cumin seeds
½ teaspoon garam masala
1 tablespoon finely chopped fresh coriander
1 teaspoon lemon juice

1 Place flour in medium bowl; rub in ghee. Add seeds; gradually stir in enough of the water to make a firm dough. Knead on floured surface until smooth and elastic, cover with plastic wrap; refrigerate 30 minutes.
2 Make potato masala filling.
3 Roll dough on floured surface until 2mm thick; cut 28 x 8cm rounds from dough. Place level teaspoons of cold filling in centre of each round; brush around edge of rounds with water, press together to enclose filling.
4 Heat oil in large saucepan; deep-fry samosas, in batches, until browned and crisp. Drain on absorbent paper.

potato masala filling Boil, steam or microwave potato until just tender; drain. Mash half of the potato in small bowl. Melt ghee in medium saucepan; cook onion, garlic, chilli, ginger, seeds and garam masala, stirring, until onion softens. Stir in coriander, juice and both mashed and chopped potato.

prep + cook time 1 hour (+ refrigeration) **makes** 28
nutritional count per samosa 2g total fat (0.7g saturated fat); 205kJ (49 cal); 6.5g carbohydrate; 1g protein; 0.4g fibre

You can also use nicola or pink-eye potatoes for this recipe.

parathas

Traditionally made with ghee and then cooked in ghee, our version uses butter in the pastry and is shallow-fried in vegetable oil. Parathas are best when cooked just before serving. You can also use nicola or sebago potatoes for this recipe.

1 cup (150g) white plain flour
1 cup (160g) wholemeal plain flour
100g cold butter, chopped
½ cup (125ml) water
300g coliban potatoes, peeled, chopped coarsely
1 tablespoon peanut oil
1 small brown onion (80g), chopped finely
1 clove garlic, crushed
½ teaspoon ground cumin
1 teaspoon coriander seeds, crushed
¼ teaspoon cayenne pepper
1 tablespoon finely chopped fresh coriander
vegetable oil, for shallow-frying

On a lightly floured surface, roll each piece of the dough into a 14cm round.

Use a 14cm plate as a guide to trim the dough into a circle.

1 Process flours and butter until mixture resembles fine breadcrumbs; add the water, pulse until mixture forms a soft dough. Wrap dough in plastic wrap; stand 1 hour.
2 Meanwhile, boil, steam or microwave potato until tender; drain. Mash in medium bowl.
3 Heat peanut oil in small frying pan; cook onion and garlic, stirring, until onion softens. Add cumin, crushed coriander and cayenne; cook, stirring, until fragrant. Add onion mixture to potato with fresh coriander; mix to combine. Cool filling 10 minutes.
4 Divide dough into 16 pieces. Roll eight pieces on lightly floured surface to form 14cm rounds (use a 14cm plate as a guide). Spread half of the filling over four of the rounds, leaving 1cm border; brush borders with water. Cover with remaining rounds; press edges together to seal. Repeat process with remaining eight dough pieces and filling.
5 Heat vegetable oil in medium frying pan; cook parathas, one at a time, until browned both sides. Drain on absorbent paper; cover to keep warm.

prep + cook time 1 hour 10 minutes (+ standing)
makes 8
nutritional count per paratha 23.4g total fat (8.5g saturated fat); 1522kJ (364 cal); 31.4g carbohydrate; 5.6g protein; 3.7g fibre

tip When you're rolling individual parathas, cover the remaining dough with a damp tea towel to stop it from drying out.

Brush the border with water before topping it with another dough round.

piroshki

6 cups plain flour (900g)
1 tablespoon dry yeast (12g)
1 tablespoon salt
⅓ cup (75g) caster sugar
2 egg yolks
2 cups (500ml) milk, warmed
250g butter, melted
1 egg, beaten lightly

beef filling

1 tablespoon olive oil
1 medium brown onion (150g), chopped finely
1 clove garlic, crushed
250g sebago potatoes, peeled, chopped finely
2 rindless bacon slices (130g), chopped finely
300g beef mince
⅓ cup (90g) tomato paste
2 teaspoons fresh thyme leaves

1 Combine flour, yeast, salt and sugar in large bowl. Make a well in the centre; using hand, mix in egg yolks, milk and butter until mixture is soft and elastic. Scrape down sides of bowl, cover; stand in warm place about 1 hour or until dough doubles in size.

2 Meanwhile, make beef filling.

3 Turn dough onto floured surface; knead until smooth. Divide dough into 16 pieces; press each piece into 12cm round.

4 Preheat oven to 220°C/200°C fan-forced. Lightly oil two oven trays.

5 Place a rounded tablespoon of the beef filling in centre of each round; gather edges, pinch firmly to enclose filling. Place piroshki, pinched-side down, on prepared trays; brush with egg. Stand, uncovered, in warm place 15 minutes. Bake, uncovered, in oven about 15 minutes or until golden brown.

beef filling

Heat oil in large frying pan; cook onion, garlic, potato and bacon, stirring, until potato softens. Add beef; cook, stirring, until changed in colour. Stir in paste and thyme. Cool 10 minutes.

prep + cook time 1 hour (+ standing) **makes** 16
nutritional count per piroshki 6.3g total fat (2.4g saturated fat); 1346kJ (322 cal); 49.9g carbohydrate; 14.2g protein; 2.8g fibre

Piroshki are small Russian dumplings that can have various savoury or sweet fillings but this one is among the most traditional. Baked or fried, they make excellent hors d'oeuvres.

white fish brandade

200g sebago potatoes, peeled, chopped coarsely
2 cups (500ml) milk
350g white fish fillet, skin and bones removed
1 small white onion (80g), chopped coarsely
2 cloves garlic, quartered
2 tablespoons olive oil
2 tablespoons lemon juice
¼ cup (60g) sour cream

1 Boil, steam or microwave potato until tender; drain. Cool.

2 Meanwhile, bring milk to the boil in large frying pan; add fish, return to the boil. Reduce heat; simmer, uncovered, until fish is cooked through, turning once during cooking.

3 When fish is cool enough to handle, flake into a food processor or blender; process with potato and remaining ingredients until mixture forms a smooth paste. Place brandade in serving bowl, cover; refrigerate 30 minutes.

prep + cook time 25 minutes (+ refrigeration)
makes 2 cups
nutritional count per tablespoon 3.7g total fat (1.5g saturated fat); 247kJ (59 cal); 2.5g carbohydrate; 4g protein; 0.2g fibre

While a classic French brandade is based on salt cod, it can be made with any fish, flaked into a garlicky sauce. We used ling here, and the resultant take on the traditional is not only just as good but easier to prepare too. Serve it with crusty bread or crackers.

cheesy potatoes

4 coliban potatoes (680g), unpeeled
1 cup (125g) coarsely grated raclette cheese
20g butter
1 tablespoon coarsely chopped fresh flat-leaf parsley
½ cup (90g) drained cornichons
½ cup (100g) drained pickled cocktail onions

1 Boil, steam or microwave potatoes until tender; drain.
2 Cut a cross in each potato, taking care not to cut all the way through; gently squeeze potatoes open. Divide cheese among potatoes; top evenly with butter.
3 Place potatoes under hot grill until cheese and butter melt. Sprinkle with parsley; serve with cornichons and onions.

prep + cook time 30 minutes serves 4
nutritional count per serving 13.8g total fat (8.6g saturated fat); 1267kJ (303 cal); 29.6g carbohydrate; 13.8g protein; 4.3g fibre

In Switzerland, this dish is known as raclette. It is a staple winter meal and is traditionally made with the pungent Swiss melting cheese of the same name. You can replace raclette with gruyère, appenzeller or even emmental. Pickled cocktail onions and cornichons are available from most supermarkets.

rosemary and potato pizza

3 medium pontiac potatoes (630g), unpeeled
1 teaspoon fresh rosemary leaves
2 tablespoons olive oil
1 cup (150g) self-raising flour
1 cup (150g) plain flour
30g butter
1 egg, beaten lightly
⅓ cup (80ml) milk
½ cup (40g) finely grated parmesan cheese
2 cloves garlic, crushed

1 Peel and coarsely chop one of the potatoes; boil, steam or microwave until tender, drain. Mash in small bowl; reserve ½ cup mashed potato.
2 Using sharp knife, mandoline or V-slicer, slice remaining potatoes into 2mm slices. Pat dry with absorbent paper. Combine sliced potato in medium bowl with rosemary and oil.
3 Preheat oven to 200°C/180°C fan-forced. Lightly oil 25cm x 30cm swiss roll pan.
4 Combine flours in large bowl; using fingertips, rub butter into flour until mixture resembles fine breadcrumbs. Add mashed potato, egg and milk; stir until combined. Turn dough onto floured surface; knead until smooth.
5 Roll dough into 25cm x 30cm rectangle; carefully lift onto prepared pan. Using palm of hand, press dough into corners of pan to ensure base is covered evenly. Top with cheese and garlic; layer potato slices, overlapping slightly, over dough. Bake, uncovered, in oven about 30 minutes or until potato is tender and pizza is browned lightly.

prep + cook time 1 hour **serves** 8
nutritional count per serving 10.8g total fat (4.2g saturated fat); 1216kJ (291 cal); 37.6g carbohydrate; 8.9g protein; 3.1g fibre

You can also use lasoda or nicola potatoes for this recipe.

roast potato and bacon quiche

300g ruby lou potatoes, peeled, chopped coarsely
1 tablespoon olive oil
1 sheet ready-rolled puff pastry, thawed
2 teaspoons olive oil, extra
1 small brown onion (80g), sliced thinly
2 cloves garlic, crushed
3 rindless bacon slices (1950g), chopped coarsely
⅓ cup (80ml) milk
⅓ cup (80ml) pouring cream
2 eggs
¼ cup (25g) coarsely grated mozzarella cheese

1 Preheat oven to 180°C/160°C fan-forced.
2 Place potato and oil in medium baking dish; stir to coat potato with oil. Roast, uncovered, about 30 minutes or until browned lightly and cooked through.
3 Meanwhile, cut pastry into four squares; gently press one square into each of four 1-cup (250ml) ovenproof dishes, lightly prick pastry with fork. Place dishes on oven tray; bake in oven 5 minutes.
4 Reduce oven temperature to 160°C/140°C fan-forced.
5 Heat extra oil in medium frying pan; cook onion, garlic and bacon, stirring, until onion softens and bacon is crisp. Drain on absorbent paper.
6 Divide potato among pastry shells; top with bacon mixture. Pour combined milk, cream, eggs and cheese into dishes. Bake, uncovered, in oven about 25 minutes or until quiche filling sets. Stand 5 minutes; carefully remove quiches from dishes.

prep + cook time 1 hour 25 minutes **serves** 4
nutritional count per serving 34.5g total fat (15.7g saturated fat); 2128kJ (509 cal); 27.8g carbohydrate; 21.2g protein; 2.3g fibre

If you find the pasty puffs up too much, just gently press it down to make room for filling. You can also use russet burbank or coliban potatoes for this recipe.

bacon and potato soup

6 rindless bacon slices (390g), chopped coarsely
4 cloves garlic, crushed
1kg king edward potatoes, peeled, chopped coarsely
1 cup (250ml) chicken stock
2 cups (500ml) water
1¼ cups (300g) sour cream
¼ cup finely chopped fresh flat-leaf parsley

1 Cook bacon and garlic, stirring, in heated oiled large saucepan until bacon is crisp.
2 Add potato, stock and the water to pan; bring to the boil. Reduce heat; simmer, covered, until potato is just tender. Add sour cream; stir until heated through (do not boil). Remove from heat; stir in parsley.

prep + cook time 45 minutes **serves** 6
nutritional count per serving 26.4g total fat (15.5g saturated fat); 1747kJ (418 cal); 24.1g carbohydrate; 20g protein; 3g fibre

You can also use bintje or pink fir apple potatoes for this recipe.

corn chowder

40g butter
1 clove garlic, crushed
1 medium leek (350g), trimmed, sliced thinly
½ cup (125ml) dry white wine
2 stalks celery (300g), trimmed, chopped finely
800g desiree potatoes, peeled, chopped coarsely
2 cups (500ml) chicken stock
2 cups (500ml) water
2 cups (320g) frozen corn kernels
½ cup (125ml) pouring cream
1 tablespoon finely chopped fresh flat-leaf parsley

1 Melt butter in large saucepan; cook garlic and leek, stirring, until leek softens. Add wine; cook, stirring, until liquid reduces by half. Add celery, potato, stock and the water; bring to the boil. Reduce heat; simmer, covered, until potato is just tender.

2 Cool 10 minutes, then blend or process 3 cups of the soup, in batches, until smooth. Return blended soup to remaining unprocessed soup; add corn and cream. Bring to the boil. Reduce heat; simmer, stirring, until corn is just tender. Remove from heat; stir in parsley.

prep + cook time 50 minutes **serves** 6
nutritional count per serving 15.8g total fat (9.8g saturated fat); 1329kJ (318 cal); 29.7g carbohydrate; 8g protein; 6.4g fibre

You can also use bintje or ruby lou potatoes for this recipe.

balsamic potato salad

1kg pontiac potatoes, unpeeled, cut into wedges
6 green onions, sliced thinly
¼ cup (35g) drained sun-dried tomatoes, sliced thinly
½ cup (75g) seeded kalamata olives
½ cup (120g) sour cream
1 tablespoon balsamic vinegar
2 tablespoons milk
½ cup firmly packed fresh basil leaves

1 Boil, steam or microwave potato until just tender; drain. Cover; refrigerate 30 minutes.
2 Combine potato in large bowl with onion, tomato and olives.
3 To make dressing, whisk sour cream, vinegar and milk in small bowl. Pour dressing over salad; toss gently to combine, sprinkle over basil.

prep + cook time 30 minutes (+ refrigeration) **serves** 4
nutritional count per serving 13.6g total fat (8.2g saturated fat); 1396kJ (334 cal); 41.3g carbohydrate; 8.5g protein; 6.3g fibre

You can also use bintje or desiree potatoes for this recipe.

dill and caper potato salad

1kg baby new potatoes, unpeeled, halved
2 tablespoons white wine vinegar
½ cup (125ml) olive oil
½ teaspoon white sugar
1 teaspoon dijon mustard
⅓ cup (65g) rinsed drained baby capers
⅔ cup (140g) drained pickled cocktail onions, halved
1 cup (200g) drained cornichons, halved lengthways
2 tablespoons coarsely chopped fresh dill

1 Boil, steam or microwave potato until just tender; drain.
2 Meanwhile, to make dressing, combine vinegar, oil, sugar and mustard in screw-top jar; shake well.
3 Combine potato in large bowl with half the dressing; cool 10 minutes.
4 Add capers, onion, cornichon, dill and remaining dressing to salad; toss gently to combine.

prep + cook time 30 minutes serves 4
nutritional count per serving 28.8g total fat (4g saturated fat); 1885kJ (451 cal); 40g carbohydrate; 6.4g protein; 5.1g fibre

You can buy pickled cocktail onions and cornichons from most supermarkets. You can also use pink fir apple or ruby lou potatoes for this recipe.

vichyssoise

50g butter
2 medium leeks (700g), trimmed, sliced thinly
750g coliban potatoes, peeled, chopped coarsely
2 cups (500ml) chicken stock
2 cups (500ml) water
300ml pouring cream
2 tablespoons coarsely chopped fresh chives

1 Melt butter in large saucepan; cook leek, covered, about 20 minutes or until softened, stirring occasionally (do not allow leek to brown).
2 Add potato, stock and the water to pan; bring to the boil. Reduce heat; simmer, covered, until potato is tender.
3 Cool 10 minutes, then blend or process soup, in batches, until smooth; place soup in large bowl. Stir in cream, cover; refrigerate 3 hours or overnight. Divide soup among serving bowls; sprinkle with chives just before serving.

prep + cook time 1 hour 10 minutes (+ refrigeration)
serves 6
nutritional count per serving 29.2g total fat (19g saturated fat); 1576kJ (377 cal); 21.2g carbohydrate; 6.3g protein; 4.1g fibre

Vichyssoise is the classic French creamy potato and leek soup that is generally served cold. You can also use desiree or pink fir apple potatoes for this recipe.

potato soufflés

350g desiree potatoes, peeled, chopped coarsely
2 tablespoons packaged breadcrumbs
60g butter
2 tablespoons plain flour
¾ cup (180ml) milk
3 eggs, separated
⅓ cup (90g) coarsely grated cheddar cheese
1 teaspoon fresh thyme leaves

1 Boil, steam or microwave potato until tender; drain. Mash potato in large bowl.
2 Preheat oven to 200°C/180°C fan-forced. Oil four ¾-cup (180ml) soufflé dishes; sprinkle bases and sides with breadcrumbs, shake out excess. Place prepared dishes on oven tray.
3 Melt butter in medium saucepan; cook flour, stirring, until mixture thickens and bubbles. Gradually add milk, stirring until mixture boils and thickens; remove from heat. Stir in egg yolks, cheese, thyme and potato, mixing until cheese melts and mixture is smooth. Return soufflé mixture to same large bowl.
4 Using electric mixer, beat egg whites in small bowl until soft peaks form. Fold egg whites, in two batches, into soufflé mixture. Spoon soufflé mixture into prepared dishes; bake, uncovered, in oven about 20 minutes or until browned lightly and puffed.

prep + cook time 1 hour **serves** 4
nutritional count per serving 25.9g total fat (15.3g saturated fat); 1517kJ (363 cal); 17.2g carbohydrate; 15.1g protein; 1.6g fibre

You can also use lasoda or sebago potatoes for this recipe.

potato, olive and sun-dried tomato bread

250g coliban potatoes, peeled, chopped coarsely
30g butter, melted
2 cups (300g) self-raising flour
1 cup (250ml) milk
½ cup (60g) seeded green olives, sliced thickly
½ cup (75g) drained sun-dried tomatoes in oil, sliced thickly
1 cup (100g) coarsely grated mozzarella cheese

1 Preheat oven to 200°C/180°C fan-forced. Oil 14cm x 21cm loaf pan; line base and sides with baking paper, extending paper 5cm over long sides.
2 Boil, steam or microwave potato until tender; drain. Mash potato in large bowl with butter until smooth.
3 Add flour, milk, olives, tomato and cheese to potato mixture; mix to combine. Spoon into prepared pan; bake, uncovered, in oven about 50 minutes or until cooked through.

prep + cook time 1 hour 15 minutes **serves** 8
nutritional count per serving 8.3g total fat (4.8g saturated fat); 1095kJ (262 cal); 35.3g carbohydrate; 9.8g protein; 3.3g fibre

You can also use nicola or pink-eye potatoes for this recipe.

boxty

900g nadine potatoes, peeled
100g butter
1 clove garlic, crushed
3 cups (450g) self-raising flour
1 tablespoon milk
2 teaspoons sesame seeds

1 Boil, steam or microwave half of the potatoes; drain. Mash cooked potatoes in large bowl until smooth. Coarsely grate remaining raw potatoes.
2 Preheat oven to 180°C/160°C fan-forced. Line two oven trays with baking paper.
3 Add butter, garlic, flour and grated potato to mashed potato; stir until mixture forms a dough.
4 Knead dough on lightly floured surface; divide into quarters. Using hands, shape each quarter into 20cm round; score a shallow cross into top of each round.
5 Place rounds on trays; brush with milk, sprinkle evenly with sesame seeds. Bake, uncovered, in oven 20 minutes. Cover with foil; bake a further 20 minutes or until cooked through.

prep + cook time 1 hour 15 minutes **serves** 4
nutritional count per serving 23.1g total fat (14g saturated fat); 3064kJ (733 cal); 109.3g carbohydrate; 17.1g protein; 8.1g fibre

Believed to have originated during the Irish famine, boxty is made of a mixture of mashed and grated potato and shaped into a thick pancake. You can also use lasoda or sebago potatoes for this recipe.

chinese potato salad

1kg pontiac potatoes, unpeeled, quartered
8 green onions, sliced thinly
5 purple shallots, sliced thinly
½ cup loosely packed fresh coriander leaves
½ cup coarsely chopped fresh mint
2 fresh small red thai chillies, sliced thinly

sesame lime dressing

¼ cup (60ml) lime juice
1 egg yolk
1 teaspoon sesame oil
¾ cup (180ml) peanut oil
2 teaspoons mirin
2 tablespoons finely chopped fresh coriander

1 Boil, steam or microwave potato until just tender; drain.
2 Meanwhile, make sesame lime dressing.
3 Place remaining ingredients in large bowl with warm potato and sesame lime dressing; toss gently to combine.

sesame lime dressing

Blend or process 1 tablespoon of the juice with egg yolk until thickened slightly. Gradually add oils in a thin, steady stream; process until mixture thickens. Stir in mirin, remaining juice and coriander.

prep + cook time 35 minutes **serves** 4
nutritional count per serving 12g total fat (2.2g saturated fat); 648kJ (155 cal); 9.5g carbohydrate; 2.1g protein; 1.3g fibre

Purple shallots are often found under the name of thai, asian or even pink shallots; used throughout South-East Asia, they are a member of the onion family but resemble garlic in that they grow in multiple-clove bulbs and are intensely flavoured. They can be eaten fresh in salads or can be deep-fried and served as a condiment.

satay chicken potato salad

1kg nicola potatoes, unpeeled, cut into wedges
2½ cups (400g) thinly sliced cooked chicken
6 green onions, sliced thinly
60g baby spinach leaves, trimmed
½ cup (70g) roasted unsalted peanuts
½ cup (150g) satay sauce
½ cup (120g) sour cream
1 tablespoon hot water

1 Boil, steam or microwave potato until just tender; drain.

2 Combine potato in large bowl with chicken, onion, spinach and half the nuts; toss gently. Drizzle with combined remaining ingredients. Serve sprinkled with remaining nuts.

prep + cook time 35 minutes **serves** 6
nutritional count per serving 26.2g total fat (10.1g saturated fat);1931kJ (462 cal); 26.2g carbohydrate; 28g protein; 5.3g fibre

You need a medium barbecued chicken for this recipe; discard skin and bones before chopping the meat. This salad can be served warm or cold. You can also use bintje or pink fir apple potatoes for this recipe.

potato varieties

bintje Oblong with a creamy skin and shallow eyes; has a yellow flesh. Good for salads and frying.

coliban Round, with a smooth white skin and white flesh. Good for baking and mashing.

desiree Long and oval with smooth pink skin and creamy yellow flesh. Good for baking, roasting and salads.

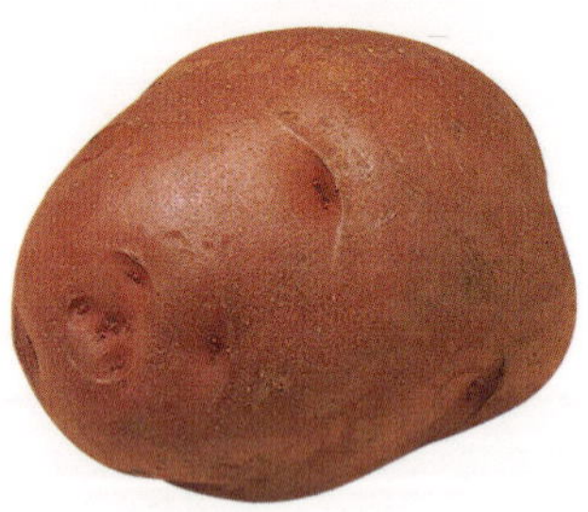

lasoda Round, with a red skin and deep eyes; has a white flesh that is good for mashing and roasting.

pink fir apple Long and knobble-shaped with a pink skin and yellow flesh. Good for roasting and salads.

nicola Oval, medium-sized potato with beige skin and a yellow flesh. Good for mashing.

nadine Small and round with cream skin and white flesh. Good in salads.

ruby lou Oval, with dark pink skin and shallow eyes; has a white flesh and is good for roasting and salads.

russet burbank A long, oval potato with rough white skin; its white flesh is good for baking and frying.

pink-eye Round potato with white skin that's pink around the eyes; its white flesh is good for mashing.

king edward Oval and kidney-shaped with a pinky white skin and white flesh. Is good for baking.

kipfler Elongated, finger-shaped potato with a yellow skin and flesh. Good for roasting and in salads.

kennebec A large, light tan potato. Its white flesh is good for frying.

purple congo Elongated, purple skinned and fleshed potato with deep eyes. Good for frying.

pontiac Round, red-skinned potato with deep eyes and a white flesh. Good for roasting and in salads.

baby new Sometimes called chats; not a variety, just an early harvest. Small, round with white skin and flesh. Good in salads.

sebago Round with a white skin and shallow eyes. Its white flesh is good for mashing and baking.

spunta Large and oblong, with a creamy skin and yellow flesh. Is good for baking and frying.

glossary

ALMOND MEAL also known as ground almonds; nuts are powdered to a coarse flour texture for use in baking or as a thickener.

BACON SLICES also known as bacon rashers; made from cured and smoked pork.

BASIL an aromatic herb; there are many types, but the most commonly used is sweet, or common, basil.

BEANS
broad also known as fava, windsor and horse beans; available dried, fresh, canned and frozen. Fresh and frozen forms should be peeled twice (discarding both the outer long green pod and the beige-green tough inner shell).
kidney medium-sized red bean, slightly floury yet sweet in flavour; sold dried or canned.

BESAN see flour.

BICARBONATE OF SODA also known as baking soda; used as a leavening agent in baking.

BREADCRUMBS
packaged crunchy, fine-textured, white breadcrumbs sold in supermarkets.
stale one- or two-day-old bread made into crumbs by grating, blending or processing.

BUTTER use salted or unsalted (sweet) butter; 125g is equal to 1 stick (4 ounces) butter.

BUTTERMILK originally the term given to the slightly sour liquid left after butter was churned from cream, today it is made similarly to yogurt. Sold alongside fresh milk products in supermarkets. Despite the implication of its name, it is low in fat.

CAPERS the grey-green buds of a warm climate (usually Mediterranean) shrub; sold either dried and salted or pickled in a vinegar brine. Baby capers are also available. Capers should be rinsed well before using.

CAPSICUM also known as bell pepper or, simply, pepper. Native to Central and South America, it can be red, green, yellow, orange or purplish black. Seeds and membranes should be discarded before use.

CASTER SUGAR also known as superfine or finely granulated table sugar.

CELERIAC a root vegetable with brown skin, white flesh and a celery-like flavour. Its soft, velvety flesh becomes creamy when mashed.

CHEESE
blue-vein mould-treated cheese mottled with blue veining. Varieties include firm and crumbly stilton types to mild, creamy brie-like cheeses.
fetta Greek in origin; a crumbly textured goat's- or sheep's-milk cheese with a sharp, salty taste.
fontina a smooth, firm cheese with a nutty taste and a brown or red rind.
goat's made from goat's milk, has an earthy, strong taste; available in both soft and firm textures, in various shapes and sizes, and is sometimes rolled in ash or herbs.
gorgonzola a creamy Italian blue cheese with a mild, sweet taste.
gruyère a Swiss cheese having small holes and a nutty, slightly salty, flavour.
mascarpone a cultured cream product made in much the same way as yogurt. It is whitish to creamy yellow in colour, with a soft, creamy texture.
pizza a blend of processed grated mozzarella, cheddar and parmesan cheeses.
provolone when young, is similar to baby mozzarella; when aged is more pronounced in flavour and hard enough to grate.
raclette a soft, sweet, Swiss cheese similar to emmental, gruyère and appenzeller.

CHILLIES
green generally unripened thai chillies, but sometimes different varieties that are ripe when green, such as habanero, poblano or serrano chillies.
jalapeno fairly hot green chillies, available bottled in brine or fresh from specialty greengrocers.
thai red small, medium hot, and bright red in colour.

CHORIZO SAUSAGE a sausage of Spanish origin, made of ground pork and highly seasoned with garlic and chillies.

CORIANDER also known as pak chee, cilantro or chinese parsley; bright-green leafy herb with a pungent flavour. Both the stems and roots of coriander are also used in cooking; wash well before using. Also available ground or as seeds; these should not be substituted for fresh coriander as the tastes are completely different.

CORNFLOUR also known as cornstarch; used as a thickening agent in cooking.

CORNICHON French for gherkin, a very small variety of cucumber.

CRÈME FRAÎCHE fresh, thick cream (with a minimum fat content of 35%) having a velvety texture and tangy taste.

CUCUMBER, LEBANESE short and slender; a popular variety due to its tender, edible skin, tiny seeds, and sweet, fresh taste.

CUMIN also known as zeera or comino; resembling caraway in size, cumin is the dried seed of a plant related to the parsley family, having a spicy, nutty flavour. Available in seed form or dried and ground.

DIJONNAISE a blend of dijon mustard and mayonnaise. It is available from supermarkets.

EGGPLANT purple-skinned vegetable also known as aubergine. Sold either raw or char-grilled and packed in oil.

FOOD MILL also known as a mouli; a rotary sieve used for liquidising and pureeing.

FLOUR

besan a fine, powdery flour made from dried, ground chickpeas; used in India for making various breads. Available from health food stores and supermarkets.

plain an all-purpose flour made from wheat.

rice a very fine flour made from ground white rice.

self-raising plain flour sifted with baking powder in the proportion of 1 cup flour to 2 teaspoons baking powder.

GARAM MASALA a blend of spices originating in North India; based on cardamom, cinnamon, cloves, coriander, fennel and cumin, roasted and ground together. Black pepper and chilli can be added for a hotter version.

GHEE clarified butter; when the milk solids are removed, the remaining fat can be heated to smoke point without burning.

GINGER also known as green or root ginger; the thick, gnarled root of a tropical plant. Can be kept, peeled, covered with dry sherry in a jar and refrigerated, or frozen in an airtight container.

GREEK-STYLE YOGURT a full-cream yogurt, often made from sheep's milk; its thick, smooth consistency, almost like whipped cream, is attained by draining off the milk liquids.

HORSERADISH CREAM a creamy prepared paste of vinegar, oil, sugar and grated horseradish.

KUMARA Polynesian name of an orange-fleshed sweet potato often confused with yam.

MACE similar to nutmeg in smell and taste, but more pungent. Typically sold in ground form. Available from spice shops.

MESCLUN a salad mix of assorted young lettuce and other green leaves, including baby spinach leaves, mizuna and curly endive.

MINCE MEAT also known as ground meat.

MIRIN sweet rice wine used in Japanese cooking; sometimes referred to simply as rice wine but not to be confused with sake, a rice wine made for drinking.

MIZUNA Japanese in origin; a feathery green salad leaf having a sharp, slightly mustardy flavour. Found on its own in most greengrocers.

OYSTER SAUCE Asian in origin, this rich, brown sauce is made from oysters and their brine, cooked with salt and soy sauce, and thickened with starches.

PANCETTA an Italian bacon that is spiced, then salt-cured, not smoked; flavourful and salty, it comes in a sausage-shaped roll and is sold sliced.

PAPRIKA ground dried sweet red capsicum (bell pepper); there are many grades and types available, including sweet, hot, mild and smoked.

PINE NUTS also known as pignoli; not really nuts, but small, cream-coloured kernels from the cones of several types of pine tree.

POLENTA (cornmeal); a flour-like cereal made of dried corn (maize), which is ground into different textures. Also the name of the dish made from it.

POTATO RICER originally a German culinary tool, a ricer is a hand-operated press, usually made of stainless steel, which extrudes potatoes and other cooked vegetables through very fine holes.

PROSCIUTTO cured, air-dried (unsmoked), pressed ham; usually sold thinly sliced.

SAMBAL OELEK (also ulek or olek) Indonesian in origin; a salty paste made from ground chillies and vinegar. Available in Asian food stores and supermarkets.

SAVOY CABBAGE is fairly bland, with a large head and crinkled dark-green outer leaves.

SICHUAN PEPPERCORNS also known as szechuan or chinese pepper, a mildly hot spice that comes from the prickly ash tree. While not actually related to the peppercorn family, its berries look like black peppercorns and have a distinctively peppery-lemon flavour and aroma.

SNOW PEA TENDRILS the growing shoots of the snow pea plant; sold by greengrocers and most supermarkets.

STAR ANISE a star-shaped, dried pod; its seeds have an astringent aniseed flavour.

SUMAC a purple-red, astringent spice ground from berries growing on shrubs that flourish wild around the Mediterranean. It adds a tart, lemony flavour to both cooked and raw foods.

TAHINI sesame seed paste available from Middle-Eastern food stores; most often used in hummus and baba ghanoush.

TOMATO

egg also called plum or roma; these smallish and oval-shaped tomatoes are much used in Italian cooking.

relish sometimes called tomato chutney; condiment made from tomatoes, onions, vinegar and various spices.

sauce also known as ketchup or catsup; made from slow-cooked tomatoes, vinegar and spices.

semi-dried partially dried tomato pieces in olive oil; softer and juicier than sun-dried, these are not a preserve so do not keep as long as sun-dried.

TORTILLA thin, round flat bread that originated in Mexico. Two kinds are available, one made from wheat flour and the other from corn (maize meal).

VINEGAR

apple cider made from fermented apples.

balsamic authentic only from the province of Modena, Italy; made from a regional wine of white Trebbiano grapes specially processed, then aged in antique wooden casks to give an exquisite pungent flavour.

rice wine made from fermented rice; colourless and flavoured with sugar and salt. Also known as seasoned rice vinegar.

V-SLICER a classic German kitchen tool used for slicing, shredding, dicing and julienning of fruits and vegetables; prized for its speed and precision.

WASABI an Asian horseradish used to make the pungent, green-coloured sauce that is traditionally served with Japanese raw fish dishes; sold in powdered or paste form.

ZUCCHINI also known as courgette; belongs to the squash family.

conversion chart

MEASURES

One Australian metric measuring cup holds approximately 250ml; one Australian metric tablespoon holds 20ml; one Australian metric teaspoon holds 5ml.

The difference between one country's measuring cups and another's is within a two- or three-teaspoon variance, and will not affect your cooking results. North America, New Zealand and the United Kingdom use a 15ml tablespoon.

All cup and spoon measurements are level. The most accurate way of measuring dry ingredients is to weigh them. When measuring liquids, use a clear glass or plastic jug with the metric markings.

We use large eggs with an average weight of 60g.

DRY MEASURES

METRIC	IMPERIAL
15g	½oz
30g	1oz
60g	2oz
90g	3oz
125g	4oz (¼lb)
155g	5oz
185g	6oz
220g	7oz
250g	8oz (½lb)
280g	9oz
315g	10oz
345g	11oz
375g	12oz (¾lb)
410g	13oz
440g	14oz
470g	15oz
500g	16oz (1lb)
750g	24oz (1½lb)
1kg	32oz (2lb)

LIQUID MEASURES

METRIC	IMPERIAL
30ml	1 fluid oz
60ml	2 fluid oz
100ml	3 fluid oz
125ml	4 fluid oz
150ml	5 fluid oz (¼ pint)
190ml	6 fluid oz
250ml	8 fluid oz
300ml	10 fluid oz (½ pint)
500ml	16 fluid oz
600ml	20 fluid oz (1 pint)
1000ml (1 litre)	1¾ pints

LENGTH MEASURES

METRIC	IMPERIAL
3mm	⅛in
6mm	¼in
1cm	½in
2cm	¾in
2.5cm	1in
5cm	2in
6cm	2½in
8cm	3in
10cm	4in
13cm	5in
15cm	6in
18cm	7in
20cm	8in
23cm	9in
25cm	10in
28cm	11in
30cm	12in (1ft)

OVEN TEMPERATURES

These oven temperatures are only a guide for conventional ovens. For fan-forced ovens, check the manufacturer's manual.

	°C (CELSIUS)	°F (FAHRENHEIT)	GAS MARK
Very slow	120	250	½
Slow	150	275-300	1-2
Moderately slow	160	325	3
Moderate	180	350-375	4-5
Moderately hot	200	400	6
Hot	220	425-450	7-8
Very hot	240	475	9

index

Published in 2010 by ACP Books, Sydney

ACP Books are published by ACP Magazines
a division of PBL Media Pty Limited

ACP BOOKS

General manager Christine Whiston
Editor-in-chief Susan Tomnay
Creative director Hieu Chi Nguyen
Designer Sarah Holmes
Senior editor Wendy Bryant
Food director Pamela Clark
Nutritional information Jordanna Levin
Sales & rights director Brian Cearnes
Marketing manager Bridget Cody
Senior business analyst Rebecca Varela
Operations manager David Scotto
Production manager Victoria Jefferys

Published by ACP Books, a division of ACP Magazines Ltd,
54 Park St, Sydney; GPO Box 4088, Sydney, NSW 2001.
phone (02) 9282 8618; fax (02) 9267 9438.

acpbooks@acpmagazines.com.au;
www.acpbooks.com.au

Printed in China by Toppan Leefung Printing Ltd.

Australia Distributed by Network Services,
phone +61 2 9282 8777; fax +61 2 9264 3278;
networkweb@networkservicescompany.com.au
United Kingdom Distributed by Australian Consolidated Press (UK),
phone (01604) 642 200; fax (01604) 642 300; books@acpuk.com
New Zealand Distributed by Netlink Distribution Company,
phone (9) 366 9966; ask@ndc.co.nz
South Africa Distributed by PSD Promotions,
phone (27 11) 392 6065/6/7; fax (27 11) 392 6079/80; orders@psdprom.co.za
Canada Distributed by Publishers Group Canada
phone (800) 663 5714; fax (800) 565 3770; service@raincoast.com

Potato favourites / food director Pamela Clark.
ISBN: 978 174245 019 3 (pbk.)
Notes: Includes index.
Subjects: Cookery (Potatoes)
Other Authors/Contributors: Clark, Pamela.
Also Titled: Australian women's weekly.
Dewey Number: 641.6521

Cover Latkes, page 42
Photographer Ian Wallace
Stylist Louise Pickford
Food preparation Amal Webster

The publishers would like to thank the following for props used in photography:
Alfresco Emporium, Village Living, Beachwood, Honeybee Homewares, Favourite Things.

To order books
phone 136 116 (within Australia) or
order online at www.acpbooks.com.au
Send recipe enquiries to:
recipeenquiries@acpmagazines.com.au